THE OLD CHURCHES OF NORWICH

JARROLD PUBLISHING

The Old Churches of Norwich, by the late Noel Spencer and Arnold Kent, was first published twenty years ago. In this edition it has been necessary to update it in view of the considerable changes which have taken place, both in the churches which are still used for worship and in those which have been declared redundant and which are now used for secular purposes.

Original text by
Noel Spencer and Arnold Kent
Revised by Alec Court
Photographs by Richard Tilbrook
Design by Michael Fuggle

ACKNOWLEDGEMENTS

In the original edition of this book Noel Spencer expressed his gratitude for the help he had received from the Norwich Public Library and Record Office and from a great many individuals. This debt of gratitude does, of course, also apply to this revised edition, and in addition thanks are due to Gordon Tilsley, Chairman of Norwich Historic Churches Trust, Kenneth Rowe, the Appeal Director, and Brian Ayers, Senior Field Archaeologist of the Norfolk Archaeological Unit, whose advice and suggestions have been of great assistance.

ISBN 0-7117-0509-7 hard covers
ISBN 0-7117-0544-5 paperback
© Jarrold Publishing 1970, 1990
First published by Jarrold Colour Publications, Norwich 1970
Revised edition published by Jarrold Publishing, Norwich 1990
Printed in Great Britain. 2/90

Introduction

IN medieval times Norwich had fifty-seven parish churches within the walls, and even today the city has more pre-Reformation churches than have the cities of London, York and Bristol put together. There are still thirty-one, and but for the last war there would be thirty-four.

They are vivid reminders of the city's age and importance, of days when rich and poor alike lived within its protecting walls and both worshipped God in the churches that stood so thick upon the ground inside the city. Even in later days, when the wealthier people had abandoned their town houses for those they had built outside, the city had remained a place where tradesmen lived over or beside their premises and the houses of the workers spread little beyond the walls.

The history of these churches goes back to times when the great religious communities – of Benedictines, Dominicans, Franciscans, Carmelites and others – occupied large areas of the city. From their stones and furnishings one can read of periods of neglect and subsequent repair and restoration, of times of prosperity when a mayor was proud to have the city's mace carried to his own particular church, and to be buried in his own parish.

They are more than just treasure houses of church art: they illustrate the changes in architectural fashion, and show the modifications that have been made to suit changes in forms of worship; from the monuments to those who were buried in these churches one can learn much of their family histories – indeed, they are a record of the social history of this part of England.

During the first half of this century there was a large decline in church membership and at the same time a considerable movement of population from the inner city to the outskirts. About 1968 a commission appointed by the Bishop of Norwich recommended that only a few of the remaining churches should continue to be used for worship. As a result of a proposal from Norwich City Council the Church Commissioners agreed to transfer to the council the freehold of each church as it was declared redundant. For its part the council undertook to preserve the fabric of each building for all time, and agreed to endeavour to find a suitable use for the premises.

To this end the council set up the Norwich Historic Churches Trust Limited – and gave it a lease of ninety-nine years on each building, the freehold remaining with the council. Sixteen churches are now in the care of the Trust and over £1 million has been spent in restoration and preservation work, this money having been contributed by the City Council, English Heritage, the Town Close Trust, and the general public who gave very generously to an appeal for funds. Most of the redundant churches have been let. In seeking suitable tenants the Trust favour socially constructive uses which respect the history and traditions of each church. It has also tried to ensure that the architectural integrity of the interiors is not impeded, but it has not been easy to find wholly sympathetic community purposes for as many as sixteen churches.

The Norwich churches are Gothic in style, a style which used the pointed arch and which, in the twelfth century, supplanted the heavy building of the Normans and persisted until the middle of the sixteenth century. The name Gothic for this kind of building was adopted by writers of the seventeenth and eighteenth centuries to describe something they considered to have been ignorant and barbarous. Indeed, it was not until the nineteenth century that a serious study was made of medieval building and the stylistic changes of the Gothic period.

The architect, Thomas Rickman, in his book *An Attempt to Discriminate the Styles of Architecture in England* (1817), seems to have been the first to give these styles the names now known so well: Early English (1150–1300), Decorated (1300–70) and Perpendicular (1370–1550). The dates are approximate, for the styles ran one into the other, the changes coming about through developments in construction and a sort of medieval 'keeping up with the Joneses'. It is to this final phase, the Perpendicular, that the bulk of the Norwich churches belong. This was the age when church builders performed their greatest feats of construction, when roofs rose to new heights yet were supported on the slenderest of walls and piers; these same walls were pierced by the largest ever windows and doors, and were reinforced by an ingenious system of buttresses. This is the greatest wonder of Perpendicular Gothic – the fact that openings have flattened arches, that roofs are low in pitch, and that window tracery has lost its branching curves and become vertical, is of secondary importance. Another feature of the Perpendicular style, to be seen in several Norwich churches, is the beautiful clerestories – those great rows of upper windows which throw light into the nave (or body) of the church, sometimes so closely set as to create an almost unbroken wall of glass.

Most of these churches are built of flint, which gives them their characteristic dark blue-toned colour. Flint is the only local building material the county has, if one excepts the rather soft brown carrstone which is found in west Norfolk. It is a difficult material to build with but was used with great skill, either roughly split to present a somewhat level surface on the outside wall when it was intended to be plastered over or, more rarely, 'knapped' into little square blocks. The combination of flint and stone which was employed to make patterns is known as flushwork and is one of the most attractive features of East Anglian church architecture. (The best flushwork in Norwich is that on the Thorpe chapel at the church of St Michael, Coslany.)

It is in their internal furnishings and arrangements that these churches have experienced the greatest changes throughout the centuries. We can try to picture their interiors in pre-Reformation days, when the great screen which stretched across the chancel, and often across the whole church, separated the clergy from the laity; and the crucifix, with its worshipping St Mary and St John, towered into the high arch of the chancel; when altars and images abounded, and the light through coloured glass could but filter into the church and turn the windows into great lighted pictures, making darker and more awesome the subjects upon the painted walls between. It is more difficult to picture, or even to believe, what happened later, for there can be no excuse for the destruction of beauty. But we have the records of those to whom any image, any picture, was an idol and who, coming to destroy, left behind them churches bereft of colour, and a trail of empty niches and headless figures.

What of these interiors in the eighteenth century – a century that had abandoned the romantic beauty of Gothic building for the cool, scholarly elegance of classical architecture and when church furnishings had been adapted to the requirements of a religion that drew much of its inspiration from the words and readings of the preacher?

Then the great three-decker pulpit dominated the church and only the bewigged parson could be seen from out of the deep box-pews which thronged the nave. There were galleries which obscured the light from the aisle windows; the altar, with its Commandment boards, was out of sight, and the chancel bare; below the chancel arch the Royal Arms had taken the place of the crucifix. The squire and his family were in their great pew, jostled by the monuments of their ancestors and, from the western gallery, the fiddlers of the choir might be heard surreptitiously tuning their instruments.

This was the Georgian church interior so much nearer to our own time, yet difficult to visualise because its destruction has been so complete. One must turn to the engravings of Hogarth or Rowlandson to see what they looked like; there are illustrations to the books of Dickens that show them too, especially an etching Phiz did for *Bleak House*, of the little church at Chesney Wold.

Complete Georgian interiors are rare in provincial Anglican churches, and not one remains in Norwich, although there are classical features in four of its churches: at St George, Colegate, St George, Tombland, St John Maddermarket, and St Helen, Bishopgate. To understand why this is so, one must look briefly at the story of that most interesting phenomenon, the Gothic Revival. Clearly the wheel of architectural change was turning back to Gothic before the eighteenth century ended. It was stimulated by those novels of terror with scenes set in ruined abbeys and castles, by the introduction of sham ruins on gentlemen's estates and by the playful use of Gothic forms as decorations applied to buildings that were, in every other respect, classical in character. From these experiments in taste, indulged in by the aristocracy, there emerged what we know as the Gothic Revival – a strange escape to medievalism at a time when the engineers of the Industrial Revolution were changing the face of Britain.

Helped along by the writings of Pugin and Ruskin it became a fashion which produced, as the nineteenth century advanced, a spate of mock Gothic offices, banks, town halls – and churches. By church architects and their clients this new fashion was taken very seriously, for the medieval style and medieval ritual had been revived together, and Gothic soon came to be considered the only form through which religious faith could be expressed. To churchmen filled with Gothic zeal, classical furnishings were anathema and there was no question of their remaining. Once again the churches were to suffer – not at the hands of image-breakers but from the activities of restorers, refurnishers and often ill-informed meddlers. The so-called 'battle of the styles', between those who favoured the Gothic and those the classical, was a hard-fought one from which Gothic emerged triumphant.

Two quotations may help to illustrate the Gothic revivalists' hatred of all things classical. Here is what the High Church journal, the *Norwich Spectator*, had to say in 1863 about eighteenth-century memorials: 'How, for instance, were inverted torches, weeping cupids,

Cherubs from the church of St Clement

urns, and the various forms of pagan sculpture pressed into the service of the Christian mourner? What possible reasons could there have been for considering little naked boys, with or without wings, appropriate upon a tomb?' The second quotation shows the same prejudice persisting as late as 1935, when W. S. Spanton, in his book *Bury St Edmunds: its History and Antiquities*, wrote: 'The Gothic builders were artists, Wren was a scientist and mathematician yet, with all his science the Cathedral [St Paul] as he rebuilt it became unsafe in two hundred years, and how inferior in beauty to the church it replaced. It was a mere copy of the work he had seen abroad, its style was foisted upon a nation whose native style of ecclesiastical architecture was in abeyance.'

Few Norwich church interiors escaped the attentions of the Gothic enthusiasts, and what one sees today is a nineteenth-century attempt to recreate the atmosphere of a fifteenth-century interior – the chancel screen restored, the chancel floor raised so that all may see the altar, the pulpit discreetly small and the choir, along with its bulky organ, brought to the eastern end of the church. The pity is that so many of these furnishings display more enthusiasm than good taste, and proclaim their period in the most strident tones.

It is easy to look back to these Victorian and Edwardian clerics and, lacking their enthusiasm, to deplore what they did in the way of restoration. But one must not forget that they breathed fresh life into the churches which had become very casual as regards their services and that, without the love and affection which they lavished upon them, many of these churches would not be with us today.

There are two free churches or chapels which must be included in this survey, for they are known throughout the country. They are the Old Meeting House (1693) and the Octagon Chapel (1756), both in Colegate. There are others which the visitor should see: the Friends Meeting House (1826) in Goat Lane and Princes Street United Reformed Church (1869).

The best examples of Puritan architecture – and the Old Meeting House and the Octagon are among them – have a charm which is all their own. Theirs is not the romance and glamour of Gothic but the qualities of modesty, good manners, and a certain domesticity. From clandestine meetings in private houses, the early Nonconformists, when they were able to build their meeting houses, chose a classical style, eminently capable of expressing that simplicity which was the essence of their religion. If the history of Puritan architecture were better known, there would be more voices raised at the disappearance of so many of its finest buildings.

All the more reason why one should see the good ones there are in Norwich.

The information contained in this book has been obtained from a study of nineteenth-century Norwich guides and directories, scrap-books and newspapers, church faculty books, photographs, drawings, and prints. They tell a story of Norwich in the not too distant past – of men and industry and their impact on the churches and the parishes in which they stood – when zealous priests were busy refurnishing their church interiors in a more 'appropriate' style, and preaching the Gospel in parishes that were ever becoming more crowded.

One learns much of men and conditions in the so-called 'good old days' of the nineteenth century, and of the problems faced by the parsons who worked in the poorer parishes. These were brave and dedicated men, struggling to do God's work and keep their churches in repair when all around was dereliction, working in places from which the wealthier people had removed themselves and had been replaced by those who became progressively poorer and more numerous, where property deteriorated, where water was at a premium, and where the graveyards rose higher and higher. For there were many churchyards which the surgeon, John Green Crosse, could describe in 1845 as 'depositories of the crumbling remains of our predecessors, accumulated to the height of many feet, and disturbed by every recent interment'. A little of this story has been set down here because it helps one to appreciate and understand what one sees in these churches.

When a church has been declared redundant most of the fixtures, monuments, wall-tablets, brasses and so on have remained in situ, but the Diocesan authorities have frequently found it necessary, in view of the new secular use, to take out the movable items. Some of these have been transferred to other churches to serve the needs of their congregations, some to the Norfolk Museums Service, and some to the Diocesan store to await a new allocation. Careful records, however, have been kept of the disposition of every item.

All Saints

IT is a far cry from the commercialised All Saints Green of today to the street in medieval times, but the old thatched former pub beside the church tower can help us to picture the kind of place it was: a street of overhanging timber houses, plastered and colourwashed, thatched or tiled. At its wider northern end was the grey tower of All Saints', its nave and chancel similarly plastered and colourwashed, and its roof of thatch; below the churchyard was the noisy, reeking Swine Market. At the southern end, where the city wall traversed what is now Queens Road, was the postern gate known as Brazen Doors and, just within, a tree-edged pond called Jack's Pit. There are houses in All Saints Green and nearby Surrey Street which provide us with another picture – of an eighteenth-century area of fashionable residences.

The southern side of All Saints' church faces down the Green: grey flint walls and roofs of lead, no aisle on this side, an unbuttressed tower (described in 1845 as 'uncommonly small', and which received its top storey in 1913) and a simple single-storeyed porch. Beside the entrance a white coffin-shaped tomb rests as though awaiting removal.

Through the porch one enters a light interior, where the Perpendicular nave windows are set in wall arches; those of the chancel are earlier, and have Decorated tracery. Nave and chancel are almost the same width and height. The tall octagonal piers of the aisle arcade lean alarmingly. A rood beam crosses the chancel arch; it bears a Latin inscription and looks very Victorian. In the south aisle there is a memorial window by F. C. Eden, dedicated in 1921.

John Morse, whose tablet is in the chancel, was a brewer of porter in St Martin at Oak; he lived in St Catherine's Close and was Mayor in 1781 and 1803. The Clabburn family who were benefactors to this and other churches are remembered by a tablet to William who died in 1812, and a slate slab which tells of Thomas's legacy to provide bread and coals for the poor of the parish.

All Saints', now in the care of Norwich Historic Churches Trust, is an ecumenical centre run by the Mothers' Union for mothers, shoppers, and visitors to the city and is open from 10 a.m. to 4 p.m. The chancel has been retained as a chapel and services are still conducted there.

St Andrew

THIS church is second in size only to St Peter Mancroft. It stands above St Andrew's Street, and looks across at another great church, the one built by the Black Friars, the nave of which is now called St Andrew's Hall, and the chancel Blackfriars Hall. The friars completed their church in 1470; St Andrew's tower was finished seven years later, and the rest by 1506. In 1539, when the friary had been dissolved, Augustine Steward was instrumental in obtaining the church 'as a fayre and large halle' for the citizens' use, and King Henry VIII for £80 granted the building to the city.

St Andrew's Street changed much in the nineteenth century. The parsonage stood where the telephone exchange now is, next door was the Royal Bazaar, opened in 1832 'for the encouragement of female and domestic industry' (where the School of Art began in 1846), and across the way was the Literary Institute and the Free Library (1822 and

Some of the coats of arms on the east wall

1857). St Andrew's Street, then called St Andrew's Broad Street, was widened at the beginning of the present century to accommodate trams.

St Andrew's church, which includes nave and chancel under one great roof, presents its northern side to the street. Its upper parts are covered in smooth stone, and the aisles have large Perpendicular windows, and two-storeyed porches that are continuous with them below a range of close-set clerestory windows.

The great flint tower has diagonal buttresses; the belfry openings and parapet may be the result of a nineteenth-century restoration. A stair-turret is on the south wall where the tower looks over Bridewell Alley. Here the churchyard once stretched to that fine old flint-walled house, now the Bridewell Museum, built by William Appleyard, who was the city's first Mayor in 1403.

As one enters through either porch, the tower walls provide clear evidence that this is a later church built against an earlier tower. It is a great hall-like interior, with soaring aisle arches supported on delicate columns, and a fine clerestory of eleven windows above. The furnishings are mid and late Victorian, and have the self-assurance of their period. The sedilia on the south of the chancel date from 1847 and the reredos from about 1850. The low stone screen separating nave and chancel, the pulpit and the pews are probably of the restoration of 1867, and the elaborate tabernacle work on the north of the chancel is

The south side and tower

Monuments to Robert Suckling *(left)* and his son, Sir John Suckling *(right)*

from 1872. The font is obviously Victorian; it replaced one sent to Walpole in 1878.

At the beginning of the nineteenth century Browne describes the interior as having an altar 'handsome but heavy, with paintings of Moses and Aaron larger than life'. He also describes a box-pewed nave with, in the centre, a pulpit (which the Reverend Dr Benjamin Ellis had erected in 1741), and before it a 'branch of 16 sockets', and at the west a 'neat organ' above a 'handsome dial', erected by parishioners in 1808.

The Suckling chapel on the north has some of the best monuments in the city. These are to the Sucklings: to Robert (Mayor in 1572 and 1582) and his son, Sir John, who died in 1613; to Francis Rugge (Mayor in 1587, 1598 and 1602); and to Robert Garsett (died 1613), of Garsett House across the way. The largest is the great Jacobean monument to Sir John Suckling and his wife, where his armoured figure reclines beside her.

Among the fine wall tablets are works by Robert Page and Thomas Rawlins: the former was responsible for that to Dr Thomas Crowe, and the latter for the two Custance tablets (one of which partially hides the blocked-up entrance to the rood stairs). Another and lesser Norwich sculptor, James Watson, carved the marble scroll, which records the parishioners' regard for their assistant curate, the Reverend Samuel Stone (the same priest who became the Vicar of St John de Sepulchre, and is commemorated by a stained-glass window in that church). The sword and mace rests are unusual in that the names of the six mayors mentioned are given in Latin. The font cover bears the date 1637; it consists of a classical entablature supported on four columns, and below it is a pierced obelisk, and above, a slender column crowned by a ball.

Five fifteenth-century panels of coloured glass have been inserted in the windows of the south aisle. Some contain heraldic shields, others show Death and the Bishop, Angels worshipping the Virgin, Abraham and Isaac ascending the Mount, and the Brazen Serpent (which is shown in blue).

Over the south-west door are canvases lettered in Gothic script which extol the virtues of the Reformation. One says that the church was 'builded of timber, stone and brick' in 1606, and has been 'lately translated from extreme idolatry'. The other declares that Queen Elizabeth has 'set up the Gospel and banished Popery'.

St Augustine

THIS church stands close to where St Augustine's Gate led through the city wall, in the north-western part of the city. When the gate was demolished in 1794 there was still much open ground round the church, for the Gildencroft, or Guild Fields, stretched to Oak Street on the west and almost to St Martin's Lane on the south. Building developments in the early nineteenth century were good (see the houses in Sussex Street and several which remain in Pitt Street), but the parish later suffered the same fate as did so many others within the walls: it became a parish of garret-workshops, of tenements and little houses and, with the coming of the railway to City Station, of larger factories.

The east end of St Augustine's church faces the street across a delightful flower-filled churchyard. Its sturdy red-brick tower, built in 1687 to replace one that had fallen down some ten years earlier, and the only one of that material in Norwich, caused the worshippers there to be known as 'Red Steeplers'. From the south, beside the Gildencroft cottages, one can observe the church's somewhat unusual proportions.

The chancel is as long as the nave, and has a steep tiled roof descending to the aisles. The nave, appearing shorter because of its height, has a low-pitched roof of lead, and a clerestory of wide-spaced Perpendicular windows.

The church was restored inside and out while the Reverend W. A. Elder was Rector (1877–1900), under Richard M. Phipson's direction: the chancel roof was 'renewed', the windows replaced and the buttresses rebuilt, a new south porch erected, the exterior walls stripped of their plaster-cement covering (a common procedure), and no doubt the Gothic battlements added to the tower.

The interior is as wide as it is long, and nave and chancel are both well lit by windows with Decorated tracery (several date from Phipson's restoration and may have replaced windows of the then unpopular Perpendicular style). There is little stained glass in the church; the small, high east window has some Victorian glass of about 1870, and a window in the north wall of the vestry is dated 1894. At the west the tall tower archway has a ringing chamber in its upper half, railed off by balusters (which came from the Georgian altar).

In the restorations which were completed in 1899 a western gallery, a pulpit and a reading desk (all of 1846) were removed, and the church was re-pewed in pitch-pine, a carved oak reredos provided, and the chancel floor raised and tiled.

A newspaper correspondent of 1900 described the interior before these changes as having 'a three-decker pulpit at the west end and a very modest little sanctuary to the eastward, being quite buried up among a wilderness of horsebox pews'.

The stately brick tower at the west end

The plain wall tablet on the south-aisle wall reminds one of the once-flourishing textile industry in the area. It is to Thomas Clabburn, who died in 1858, and was erected by '600 of his weavers'. This gentleman was the head of Clabburn, Son & Crisp, the most important textile firm in Norwich at that time, makers of 'shawls in every variety, and also paramattas, bareges, tamataves, balzarines, poplins, fancy robes, and grenadines etc.'. Clabburn's factory was probably quite small, and the 600 weavers outside workers, for, to quote a contemporary writer: 'Most of the weavers work for the firm at their own houses, and there, in humble dwellings, produce the beautiful fancy fabrics which are destined to adorn the daintiest ladies in the land.'

Matthew Brettingham, the architect (1699–1769), is commemorated by a large tablet in the vestry. He worked on several great East Anglian houses, including Holkham, Benacre, Gunton and Langley.

St Benedict

BAYNE, writing of St Benedict's church in 1869, says that it had recently been 'repaired and re-roofed at the cost of £180'. The fabric was again repaired in 1896, for it had become 'dilapidated and dangerous', a large elderberry tree was growing out of the tower, and kestrel hawks had taken to nesting there.

This little church had a single north aisle, north and south porches and, curiously enough, an aisle arcade supported on slender cast-iron columns. It was situated midway between Pottergate and St Benedict's Street, with small churchyards on north and south, and access from either street. For the rest, the church was hemmed in by a multitude of little properties, and larger houses which had become tenements, stretching to the city wall on one side and to Ten Bell Lane on the other.

That was St Benedict's until one night in 1942 when German bombs descended upon this crowded little parish and swept much of it out of existence; they destroyed the church and left only the tower. That is all one sees today – a round tower with an octagonal top and a pyramid roof – standing upon a neat lawn and providing an attractive and striking feature in the midst of the modern dwellings which have replaced the houses of Neal's Square and Duck Lane and the byways in between. The round portion of the tower is probably Norman and the octagonal upper storey, a feature of several East Anglian round towers, may date from the fifteenth century.

In 1972 excavation of the whole church site was undertaken, conducted by J. P. Roberts of the Norfolk Museums Service, before mass exhumation of the human remains in the church and churchyard was carried out, so that the site could be developed for housing. Evidence was found of an eleventh-century church and of the addition of a west aisle in the following century. Many interesting artefacts were discovered, including medieval pottery sherds.

All that remains of St Benedict's

St Clement

THERE were rejoicings in Colegate in 1795, and the parishioners of St Clement's erected a grand triumphal arch at the east end of the church, to celebrate the election of Alderman Jeremiah Ives as Mayor of the city for the second time. The arch was illuminated at night, and must have stretched across Colegate to the large Georgian house which had been the Mayor's family home. He was the last but one of a number of Jeremiah Ives to occupy this position between 1733 and 1801. The old Ives house later became a rectory, and its large garden at the rear is now a car park. But one can still stand beside the walls of this house and look across at the church where Jeremiah was buried – the church of St Clement the Martyr – said by many writers to be the oldest in the city.

It is a rather ordinary little church with a beautiful tower. The nave is short and wide, the chancel lower and narrower; both are of flint with slated roofs of low pitch. The four-storeyed tower, also of flint, is tall and slender and appears even more so from the north (Colegate) side because of the stair-turret. There is a clock with a handsome classical surround upon the eastern face. Above the square sound-holes are fine Perpendicular belfry openings and a tall parapet, battlemented and decorated with flushwork lozenges. At the base of the tower is a door to the stair-turret.

The plan of the church is exceedingly simple. It has neither aisles nor porches, and only small entrance doors, with a window over, on both north and south. With the exception of the little vestry attached to the chancel's northern side, the church appears the same on north and south, two Perpendicular windows lighting the nave, and one the chancel. The east wall of the chancel stands in Fye Bridge Street, and has a Decorated window of medium size. On three sides of the church is its walled burial ground, almost devoid of memorials save for a white box-tomb which stands rather lonely, on the south. This is a nineteenth-century rebuild of the tomb erected to his parents by Matthew Parker, Chaplain to Anne Boleyn and to Henry VIII, and Archbishop of Canterbury under Elizabeth.

Now the interior. One enters by the north door and reaches the nave through a wooden vestibule. The nave is short and wide, the chancel much lower and narrower. The whole church is light, for there is no stained glass, save for a little colour in the surround of the east window. The timbers of the roof descend onto wall posts and, in the chancel, these not only carry angels but have connecting arch braces upon the walls, above windows set in wall arches.

At the west end a tall arch opens into the tower, the foot of which has been screened off to form a little vestry. Within this another door leads to the tower stairs. The font is octagonal, with flowers and leaves on the bowl, and is

The south side and fine Perpendicular tower

The wall tablet of Jeremiah Ives, who died in 1741

attributed, by Cautley, to the sixteenth century. On the nave floor is a brass to Margaret Pettwode, dated 1514.

Throughout the eighteenth and into the nineteenth century the Ives and Harveys have spread their memorial tablets upon the walls. From them we can piece together bits of the history of these two ancient families, who came from elsewhere and achieved importance in the life of the city. The Ives were wool merchants, the Harveys merchants, manufacturers and bankers who established the firm of Harvey and Hudson, and both families became linked by marriage.

The earlier tablets have pilasters, scrolls and cherubs. That to John Harvey, Mayor in 1727, (on the south wall), is of this kind, and bears an inscription which states that, 'by his assiduous application and exact economy he acquired an ample fortune'. On the north wall a similar tablet describes the last illness of poor Jeremiah Ives who, in 1733, was the first mayor of that name and who died in 1741, having 'for three years endured the torture of the stone with invincible fortitude of mind'. The memorial to his son Jeremiah, who died in 1805 and who has already been mentioned in connection with the house across the way, is a very plain affair and, strangely, does not mention his mayoralties. Other mayors or 'Fathers of the City' as they seem to have called themselves – the Harveys provided eight – are remembered upon these walls. Their memorials are interesting as pieces of sculpture, for one can trace their decline from baroque exuberance to classical dullness.

Since passing into the care of Norwich Historic Churches Trust, St Clement's has become a pastoral and counselling centre run by a Methodist minister. Repairs and renovation, especially to the tower, have recently been completed.

The light interior, looking west

13

St Edmund

THIS small church stands in Fishergate, on a fragment of churchyard with its north side facing the street. It is a humble building of flint with nave and chancel combined under one long roof, a single-storey porch and vestry on the side, and a stalwart tower at the west which has deep diagonal buttresses that end where the belfry stage begins. Tall buildings surround the church on three sides; on the south side is the only aisle, running the length of the building and with no clerestory above it. Here the tower has a stair-turret.

The stalwart tower at the west end

The nave, chancel and the wide aisle are well lit by their Perpendicular windows. They light a few good tablets that remain upon the walls, and the boss on the nave roof that has the emblem of St Edmund. But the most interesting feature of this interior is the curious arrangement of openings which forms the aisle arcade: openings of various heights and widths with pieces of solid wall at intervals.

The architect Edward Boardman had been responsible for destroying the Georgian furnishings and substituting Gothic in 1882, and Robert Flood has written of the old interior he knew in his youth. He tells how, within a wooden enclosure at the east end of the aisle, worshippers sat round a Cromwellian table to receive their Communion.

This parish, and the neighbouring one of St James, was where, early last century, certain Norwich businessmen made a gallant but belated attempt to save the rapidly declining textile trade. Even by the end of the eighteenth century the thrusting, enterprising textile men of the Yorkshire towns, so different from the 'gentlemen' employers of East Anglia, had outstripped them in production and were undercutting them in price. Not only had the northerners been quicker to mechanise production, but they had the raw materials of power upon their doorstep. In 1833 Mayor Samuel Bignold formed the Norwich Yarn Company which, in six years, built three large steam-powered factories, each having several floors to rent to individual firms. The first was raised upon an orchard beside St Edmund's church in 1834, a second was built in 1836, and a third, in St James's parish, in 1839. They came too late, for by 1845 Norfolk had still only 428 power-looms compared with Yorkshire's 31,000. Only one of the buildings remains, the handsome one in St James's parish, now part of the Jarrold printing works. The fire which destroyed the factory beside the church one January night in 1913 provided the watchers on Quayside with a never-to-be-forgotten spectacle.

For some decades the church was used for storage and was sadly neglected, so that when the Norwich Historic Churches Trust assumed responsibility it was a broken-down pigeon-infested hulk. A major restoration has been completed and this attractive little church now awaits a sympathetic secular tenant.

St Etheldreda

TOWARDS the southern end of King Street, not far from where the city wall descends from Ber Street towards the Boom Towers, there are two churchyards. On one are fragments of a tower, which are all that remains of the church of St Peter Southgate, and on the other is the church of St Etheldreda.

In 1884 St Peter's was in bad repair and the Vicar (the Reverend Nathaniel Bolingbroke) obtained a faculty to 'dilapidate' it, which meant that it was to be allowed to become a ruin, and to disperse its contents, and this was done. Today the churchyard is used as a children's playground.

St Etheldreda's sits upon its shaded churchyard, a venerable church with walls of flint, steep tiled roofs and a tower that rises only a little above the ridge of the nave. The nave roof retained its thatch longer than any other city church, losing it only in 1883 when Edward Boardman restored the church. Several new windows were inserted at that time, and there is mention of a rood-stair being uncovered. During restorations in 1855 wall-paintings are recorded as being found, including a 'gigantic' St Christopher close to the north door and a Trinity in the splays of certain windows on the same side. The ancient tower is a pretty combination of flint and bright red brick, its lower part a plain cylinder of flint, and its upper part a flint octagon with brick angles and belfry surrounds. The blocked-up northern entrance to the nave has the remains of a Norman arch above it, and strips of Norman masonry beside it.

Norwich Historic Churches Trust has restored the tower and renewed the roof; at the same time north lights have been inserted for the enthusiastic band of sculptors and artists who occupy the church. They themselves have imaginative plans for improving the interior as studios, and in the meantime make use of the churchyard for the display of their sculpture.

St George Colegate

IN the eighteenth century the textile industry of Norwich achieved its greatest prosperity. Of the men who controlled that industry, the master weavers, a contemporary observer wrote thus: 'Being opulent men, and generally surrounded by their dependants, they have something of a lordly bearing.' These were the men who lived in the large houses still to be seen in and around Colegate, and together with their 'dependants' attended one or other of the places of worship in that street.

St George Street, once called Gildengate because it led to the Gildencroft, crosses Colegate, and the church of St George stands at this crossing. There are several recorded dates of its building – the nave and tower

Detail from spandrel over the south door

came first, about 1459, the chancel about 1498, then in 1505 the north aisle was added and finally, in 1513, that on the south. The church's grime-darkened exterior is impressive. It has a tall, buttressed tower, a high rather short nave with close-set clerestory windows and a low-pitched roof, a chancel that is lower and narrower, and aisles on either side with a two-storeyed porch attached to that on the south.

The interior is exciting and different, for the church is fortunate in having retained a good deal of Georgian woodwork which takes its place so happily in this Gothic fabric; indeed, one sees here Georgian furnishings which have been removed from most Norwich churches. Entering from the west, one passes between the columns supporting a classical gallery, built for the choir, on which now stands the delightful little organ, a fine instrument, purchased in 1802, and wisely moved back from the north aisle in recent years. The pews in the nave are still those that were put here in the late eighteenth or early nineteenth century, and very handsome and dignified they look.

One can admire the fine Georgian reredos behind the altar, and the magnificent pulpit, with its high sounding-board, at the entrance to the chancel. Look at the memorials – even at those black grave slabs that pave the church – some with names cut so large and so deep that they can never be forgotten. One beside the fourteenth-century font tells of the

'The pews in the nave are still those that were put here in the late eighteenth or early nineteenth century'

death of poor Bryant Lewis, murdered on Thetford Heath in 1698. The earliest tomb is one in terracotta, to Robert Jannys (Mayor in 1517 and 1524). A window at the east was covered to erect Bacon's graceful tablet to 'Honest John Herring', somewhat inappropriate for this Mayor of 1799 who was known for his bluntness of speech and manners.

John Crome (1768–1821), landscape painter and founder of the Norwich Society of Artists, worshipped at St George's and was buried in the church.

17

St George Tombland

ONE can come upon this church from Princes Street where its tower looks so picturesque above the old houses, or from where its southern side is seen among the trees of Tombland. This is St George Tombland – a venerable-looking church, which stands upon a little triangle of churchyard.

The open space called Tombland is of great antiquity. Before the Castle or Cathedral came, this was a Saxon market, conveniently near the river and an ancient crossing. The Norman conquerors considered that such a place where people met would be better situated near the walls of the castle they were building. So Tombland market was moved and much of its ground disappeared under the buildings of the Benedictine monastery and its great cathedral church. But it long remained a place for buying and selling, the scene of frequent bloody disputes between monks and citizens and, until 1744, the site of the famous Tombland Horse Fair.

St George's church, once called St George at the Gates of the Holy Trinity, was built here in the middle of the fifteenth century. It is an attractive church, whether seen from Tombland or from quieter Tombland Alley. The handsome tower beside the alley has diagonal buttresses, a stair-turret on its north side and a pretty blue clock face on its south. East of the tower the nave – roofed with lead and once of higher pitch – has a clerestory of widely separated windows with, surprisingly, walls of brick between (remarked upon as long ago as 1840).

The southern side seen through the trees of Tombland

There are aisles on north and south and the flint chancel, which is lower, has some late Perpendicular windows whose arches have no curves whatever. It is entered by a priest's door on the south. Projecting from the south aisle, and rising a little above it, is a pleasant two-storeyed porch of flint. It has a window above the entrance, flushwork in the gable and a small stair-turret on its west side. This porch was restored in 1890; a painting by Henry Ninham shows one of much less conventional design, with three niches upon the front and strange, baluster-like angle buttresses. There is another two-storeyed porch on the north side which is set alongside the aisle.

The interior is not spectacular; the nave is short and wide, the chancel long and of almost the same width. This is not an interior where delicate soaring piers support a clerestory of glass. Here the tall, pointed aisle arches rest on pillars that are short and heavy, with much more wall above them, and windows that are less closely set. The fine timber roof has long wall posts, and upon those in the chancel, looking like birds poised for flight, are winged angels holding shields.

At the entrance to the chancel and behind the altar are two fine features that have survived from the Georgian church. The pulpit, approached by a delicate staircase, has delightfully carved panels inlaid with ivory and is reminiscent of the pulpit at St George Colegate. The reredos is one of the best of its period in Norwich; it is more elegant than the one at St George Colegate, but less splendid than the great baldacchino at St John Maddermarket. The octagonal bowl of the thirteenth-century font is supported on a cylindrical shaft, round which eight little pillars were placed during the restoration of 1879–86.

Descriptions of the changes in the church's furnishings during these years give us the date of much else that one sees. A writer in 1852 had described the interior as 'somewhat crowded with pews and galleries'. Edward Tillett, writing in 1891, tells us that galleries at the west end of the nave were removed, and the old high pews destroyed to make way for the present oak benches.

The organ was, no doubt, put into the east end of the north aisle at the same time – jammed in would be a better description, for so tightly is it fitted that one wonders whether these Victorian organs were bought 'off the peg', so frequently are they ill adapted to the

The pulpit and chancel

spaces they occupy. This one is within a few inches of the aisle window which is filled with stained glass, above a mouldering brass plate, both in memory of a rector named Sutton, who died in 1846, after ministering here for fifty years.

There are several good memorial tablets in the church. At the west end are sword and mace rests with the names of Mayors John Press (1753), Jeremiah Ives Junior (1786) and John Steward (1810). There is an alabaster relief (which Pevsner considers to be German, of about 1530), a seventeenth-century font cover, a statuette of St George and the Dragon, and Victorian stained glass.

St Giles

THE handsome street of St Giles runs from the City Hall to St Giles Gate, where until 1792 was the gate in the city wall. The street lies along the northern edge of a plateau which drops away towards the river and where, lower down, are the churches of St Gregory, St Laurence, St Margaret and St Swithin. Many of its fine Georgian houses were once the homes of medical men, whose memorials appear upon the walls of St Giles' church.

St Giles' stands on the north side of the street. It has a great 120-foot tower that is not only the tallest in Norwich but rises from the highest ground. This tower dominates the river valley to the north and the entrance to the city on the west, and was indeed a beacon tower, for the iron basket which held the fire is still preserved within the church. It is an unusual tower in that it has eight buttresses, two down each angle, which are set at right-angles to the wall faces. The nave and aisles are late fourteenth century, the porch attached to the south aisle is a century later, and the chancel and north vestry are nineteenth century. With the exception of the highly ornamental ashlar front of the porch all the walls are of flint, those of the chancel being knapped.

The clerestory windows are widely spaced, with one above each window of the aisle; the chancel, much lower than the nave, has space above its roof to allow for a small window in the nave gable. This Decorated chancel and the vestry attached to it were added between 1866 and 1867 when considerable restorations were carried out under the direction of R. M. Phipson. (The then incumbent, the Reverend W. N. Ripley, seems to have borne most of the cost of erecting it.) St Giles' had been without a chancel since 1581, when Dean Gardiner, to save the Dean and Chapter the expense of

The tallest church tower in Norwich

keeping it in repair, had ordered that it be demolished and the materials given to the parish for 'a stock to be put out for the encouragement of poor traders'.

The roof within the porch has a beautiful fan vault, the only one in Norwich, and passing under this one enters the south aisle. The arches that open into the nave are both wide and high and, supported on delicate piers, rise close to the clerestory windows. A fine hammer-beam roof of early and unusual form covers the nave, one where the arch braces climb from deep wall posts to the angels of the hammer-beam and thence continue the same curve to the ridge of the roof. The great arch that opens into the chancel has three niches down either side and is, undoubtedly, the original one; the east window, with its flamboyant tracery, is filled with good stained glass given by Sir Peter Eade in 1904. (Sir Peter, a surgeon, then living at Churchman House, wrote a comprehensive history of the church and parish.)

The window at the end of the south aisle was subscribed for by his students to the memory of John Godwin Johnson, a surgeon and Mayor of the city in 1855.

One cannot here do justice to the wall monuments which are very good indeed. The only tablet in East Anglia by Sir Henry Cheere is that to Alderman Thomas Churchman (1742) and there are two by Thomas Rawlins – to Philip Stannard (1747) and to Sir Thomas Churchman (1781).

There are two large brasses in the nave floor: to Robert Baxter (Mayor 1424), and to Richard Purdaunce (1436). In the south aisle is a chalice brass to John Smyth (1499). From Phipson's plans for the restoration (shown on the church wall) one can see exactly what was

'The arches ... are both wide and high'

done between 1866 and 1867. Sir Peter Eade's book gives details of the Georgian interior, high-backed pews, classical reredos and west gallery. It describes the restoration – the new chancel paved with Minton tiles, the new seating, and the lighting of the church 'by means of eight five-branched gas standards, and other smaller wall branches'.

Left: '...the porch has a beautiful fan vault'
Right: '...The only tablet in East Anglia by Sir Henry Cheere'

21

St Gregory

ST Gregory's is a fascinating and unusual church which, because of its position on a similar sloping site, and its north and south porches, somewhat resembles its neighbour, St Andrew's.

Externally a little grim, it is a smaller, humbler edition of St Andrew's, for its builders used no ashlar facings upon its walls but left them all of flint. Its low tower lost its spire, a Norwich landmark, in 1840.

One of the fascinations of St Gregory's is the way in which the tall east end is built out over an alley, which slopes steeply down from Pottergate. This right-of-way seems originally to have been the bed of a stream and later part of a processional way round the church.

St Gregory's is best seen from the south, where a delightful little square of grass (the former churchyard) separates it from Pottergate. The unbuttressed tower has a large Decorated belfry opening. The tall aisle windows are Perpendicular, while the close-set windows of the clerestory are of the Decorated style; the whole church is roofed in lead.

The aisle ends near where the sanctuary extends across the passage, and tucked in beside it is a priest's door and a tiny vestry. Above the vestry a great Perpendicular window provides light for the chancel.

The two-storeyed porch has a pinnacled niche over the door and, above it, a clock in a classical surround. One enters the church through this porch, under a vaulted roof ornamented with bosses that show St Gregory instructing a music class, and a martyr led to execution.

The interior is light and spacious, nave and chancel continuing, without chancel arch, from west to east.

The nave is short but immensely high and wide, and so slim are the piers of the arcades that nave and aisles appear as one. The arcades end at the sanctuary, which is raised on seven steps to give clearance for the passage beneath (and for a crypt which was later used as a charnel place). It is an impressive east end. The steps rise to a simple altar with a wall of panelled stone behind it and an enormous window above (filled with rather poor glass of 1864).

In 1861, R. M. Phipson, who was then said to have been engaged in restoring between twenty and thirty churches in Norfolk and Suffolk, was commissioned to undertake work here. The Vicar, the Reverend W. R. Sharpe, had already made certain changes, including the installation of a new organ at the east end of the north aisle. Phipson seems to have made the usual alterations – removing the pulpit, reredos, pews and west gallery, and substituting much of the furnishings that one sees today.

When Mr Sharpe left the church two years later, he was succeeded by a man of very

The south porch and tower

'...a fine octagonal font with a panelled stem'   The church is now used as a centre for music and the arts

different views, the Reverend J. Wortley. This gentleman did not find favour with the writers of the High Church journal the *Norwich Spectator*, and month by month during 1864 its contributors became more and more angry at what the new vicar was doing. First they had no wish to reproach him but 'regretted', then they wrote of his intention to undo the work of restoration, of his desire that the church should 'resume the aspect of a modern meeting house' and of 'despoilers' at work. When the Vicar returned the organ to the west, they had this to say: 'The organ was displaced for the sole reason that it concealed the very ugly bust of a man in armour with a flowing wig, intended to represent Sir Peter, the benefactor.'

The organ must have remained at the west end for several years for the memorial window to the Reverend John Jessop was put in the north-east chapel in 1883. Now it is marooned behind the present organ along with the 'ugly bust' referred to by the *Spectator*. This grubby but fine monument, by Thomas Green, of Camberwell, on which is a half-figure holding a baton, is to Sir Peter Seaman (Mayor in 1707), a brewer, whose family house was on the site of Bullard's brewery.

St Gregory's has several treasures. It has a fine octagonal font with a panelled stem and shields upon the bowl. The latter is supported by eight angels which look down upon the same number of strange monsters, apparently crushed beneath the stem, which symbolise the carnal desires of the flesh, driven out at baptism. There are several fine monuments, the best being the Bacon monument (1659) in the south-east corner of the nave, and this has recently been restored by Norwich Historic Churches Trust. A large fifteenth-century wall painting of St George was uncovered in the north aisle in 1861 when the organ was moved and this is shortly to be restored by the Trust. Other traces of medieval paintings have recently been found in the south aisle.

A beautiful eagle lectern of 1496, a sanctuary knocker, and a baroque crucifix which hung above the pulpit were all removed when the church was declared redundant.

Norwich Historic Churches Trust has carried out substantial works of restoration to the main structure and St Gregory's has now been converted into a centre for music and the arts, principally for amateur performers. St Gregory's Trust has been established to further the work of the centre.

St Helen

JUST outside the cathedral precinct, in Bishopgate Street, is that fascinating cluster of buildings which comprises the Great Hospital, and its church of St Helen.

The long history of the Great Hospital begins in 1249, when it was founded by Bishop Suffield as a place where, under the charge of a Master, four chaplains were to celebrate Masses, and pray for the soul of the Bishop. It was further to give asylum to infirm clergy, and food (which could be eaten by the fire in winter) to thirteen old people, and to seven poor scholars during term time.

The church that Bishop Suffield began to build upon the Hospital grounds took the place and the name of one that stood opposite, within the cathedral precinct, and the church we know today serves not only the Hospital, but also the parish of St Helen's. The Hospital,

well endowed by its founder, continued to receive considerable gifts of land and property throughout the centuries that followed. Of the Bishop's original church, only the vaulted roof of the south porch remains. The present chancel was erected by Bishop Despencer about 1380, and the rest of the church was rebuilt by Bishop Goldwell about a century later. During that time the nave was extended to provide an Infirmary Hall with a great window at its western end and, beside it, a tower attached to the south aisle. At this end, too, a Refectory was built against the north aisle, along with a delightful little cloister and, towards the east, the south aisle received its transept.

The Hospital continued its work in accordance with the rules of its foundation until the reign of Henry VIII when, along with other monastic institutions, it fell into the hands of the king. Although Henry seems to have been persuaded to hand the buildings over to the city, for them to become a place for the relief of the sick poor, it was left to his son, the young Edward VI, to carry this out; in 1547 ownership of the Hospital and its properties was transferred to the mayor, sheriffs, and citizens of Norwich.

Before the end of the century the interior of the great church had been divided up to provide wards for the inmates. The chancel divided horizontally into two storeys became the women's wards, and the bulk of the nave was similarly divided to provide wards for the men; the space between was sealed off and remained a place of worship. Three of these old wards have now been converted to general purposes, but the fourth has been retained to give an indication of life as it used to be in the hospital.

One can enter the church either by the south porch or from the cloister on the north. The latter is such a charming place that one might choose to approach the church that way; it is a cloister in miniature, with square-headed openings that look upon a courtyard of green.

The church's square interior, surprisingly small, comprises the three eastern bays of the nave, with aisles on either side, and a transept on the south-east. The chancel arch is walled across, and a wall on the west seals off the rest

The vaulted roof of the transept

'... a delightful little cloister'

of the nave. The aisle arches are high pitched, with clerestory windows over them, and they rest on graceful quatrefoil piers. All the windows are of the Perpendicular style, one on the south having vertical mullions only, and no tracery. The church's finest feature is the vaulted roof of the transept which Pevsner describes as 'a sumptuous lierne vault, close in style to the vaults of the cathedral but different in pattern'. The bosses at the intersections of the ribs are beautifully carved and their colours were renewed in the 1950s. On the centre boss is the Coronation of the Virgin, and the major bosses that surround it show the Annunciation (N), the Resurrection (S), the Nativity (E) and the Ascension (W). The intermediate bosses show Saints Catherine, Edward, Edmund and Margaret, and the outer bosses the named twelve Apostles.

The furnishings add to the fascination of this interior, for there are box-pews on three sides, and open benches in the centre. These are deep box-pews, each with a door, and, at the east end, they mass together to surround a two-decker pulpit. Upon the wall behind is a very large framed painting described as a copy of Raphael's *Transfiguration*, made in the Vatican for Thomas Kerrick, of Geldeston Hall, High Sheriff of Norfolk 1778–9. In the transept is the box-pew that William Ivory was permitted to erect in 1780 to be 'convenient for his family and servants'. Opposite this, behind a Victorian rail, is a Stuart altar table and, above it, a fine classical reredos, painted with the Commandments, Creed and Lord's Prayer.

Among the box-pews along the north wall is a small organ in a pretty Gothic case (dated 1881). Most of the nave benches have poppy-heads upon their arms, but two at the east end have carved animals and figures (probably sixteenth century). On the ground the black grave-slabs of former parishioners crowd towards the east, where, among the Attesleys, Dyballs, and Reynolds, appears the name of the Norwich antiquary, John Kirkpatrick, who died in 1728, when only 42.

The tall sword and mace rests bear only one name, that of Peter Thacker, Mayor in 1705. Among the possessions of St Helen's is an interesting chained bible.

St James

A painting of about 1820 by David Hodgson gives us a vivid picture of the church of St James, and the Pockthorpe area, as he knew it. It shows Barrack Street lined with ancient gabled houses that threaten to fall into it, a street that has little paving and no pavements, inhabited by people of the poorest sort, and a dog that forages in the open drain.

About the same time, Henry Ninham painted the Cathedral, seen from Cowgate, then a narrow street of gabled houses, shops and pubs. In 1857 Mrs Madders, in Fletchers' *Norwich Handbook*, described the same view. 'Passing down this Street,' she wrote of Cowgate, 'we have one of the most picturesque street views the city affords with the spire of the Cathedral in the distance forming the close to the long vista of gable ends and projecting storeys. Two towering factories rise on either hand of you at the end of the street. That on the left is leased out to various manufacturers by the Yarn Company, by whom it was built, so that an immense amount of machinery, worked by steam power, is applied to a variety of different purposes. A large quantity of gauze crape amongst other articles is manufactured here. The factory on the right is exclusively devoted to the spinning of mohair, and is the property of Robert Wiffin Blake Esq.'

The left-hand factory in this description is the one now occupied by Jarrold Printing, which has also preserved a fragment of a much older building, an arch of the Carmelite or Whitefriars Friary that occupied the area between here and St James's church from 1256 until the Dissolution.

The little church of St James has a strange tower, one of brick that stands not beside but upon the church. But it is a tower and not a turret – in shape a cube with an octagon upon it. A photograph of 1909 shows St James's standing upon a large churchyard, against the wall of which is a Victorian drinking fountain. It shows, too, the south porch front surmounted by a classical pediment with three figures perched upon it. Today only the southern churchyard remains. The roof of the nave covers the only aisle in one great sweep; there are large Perpendicular windows on the west and north (where there is also a rood stair-turret and a small entrance door).

Beyond is a wide nave with a shallow, scissor-beam roof from which broad arches open into the aisle (the piers lean alarmingly but are said to have done so for more than 200 years). The square chancel, narrower than the nave, has a Decorated east window which contains some good fifteenth-century Flemish glass. The wall tablets are few and small, the best being that to Nicholas Emmes (1632).

St James's, long situated in a slum parish dominated by the great Pockthorpe brewery and the Nelson barracks (built to house 320 men and 266 horses), seems to have received little attention from nineteenth-century restorers, although one knows that work was carried out here in 1842, and again in 1882.

All the furnishings of St James's have now been removed and the building transformed into a delightful puppet theatre. On the south side an octagon has been constructed to provide storage and working space. The architect for the whole complex was the firm of Peter Codling.

'... a cube with an octagon upon it'

St John Maddermarket

THIS church stands in an area of narrow ways which teem with the history of old Norwich and of its once famous woollen trade. The name Maddermarket tells what went on here, as does the street called Charing (or Shearing) Cross – the latter the place where the Dukes of Norfolk built their great palace – and where even in 1681 the palace grounds were said to be hemmed in by 'tradesmen's and dyers' houses who foul the river water by their constant washing and cleaning their cloth'. Close by is the house we know as Strangers' Hall, where in 1565 the Sothertons brought master workmen, 'strangers', from the Low Countries to assist them in the making of fabrics. St John's is essentially Perpendicular; the clerestory of close-set windows above the aisles, the low-pitched roofs, and the windows with flattened arches and vertical tracery all declare it to be so. It is a short church – as wide as it is long – where the absence of a chancel poses a question: why, if it ever had one, has the east end a Decorated window which would seem to be a century earlier?

The tower – sparkling with white stone among the flints and with the four evangelists upon its parapet – is beautiful. It is best seen from the north, where it broods over narrow Maddermarket Alley, and provides one of the most attractive views in Norwich. An arch under the tower leads into the alley, where one sees the unusual north porch, and the most unsuitably placed parish pump at its foot.

Inside, the western end is darkened by a gallery overhead and shut off from the rest of the church by a gated screen. The nave beyond is short and high and leads, past slender piers, into the aisles. The east end is exciting, for a splendid east window filled with Victorian glass has below it a handsome eighteenth-century baldacchino, a mahogany Communion rail and a double-sided lectern of the same wood. The Communion rail and lectern seem to have been put here by the Reverend William Busby who was Rector from 1898 to 1923 (and no doubt lived in the Gothic rectory in Unthank Road, opposite Park Lane). The pews, pulpit (described as 'chaste' when installed) and font belong to the restorations of 1864 and 1876.

There is a little chapel on the north enclosed by screens, one Gothic, one Jacobean. The style of the latter appears again in the large western screen which, surprisingly, was erected in 1912.

There are monuments in the south aisle to the sixteenth-century Mayors of Norwich the Layers and the Sothertons. One more memorial must be noted – that to Lady Margaret, Duchess of Norfolk, which is high up between the north aisle arches. The Duchess died in 1563 while on a visit to the Duke of Norfolk's palace and was buried in the north aisle of this church – not until 1791 was

'St John's is essentially Perpendicular'

her memorial erected. Records tell how the Duchess was brought to St John's from the palace, of the great procession of Church and civic dignitaries, and of lords and ladies which accompanied the body of this lady, the second wife of the greatest nobleman in the land. Her effigy lies on the great tomb in Framlingham church, prepared for the Duke, along with that of his first wife. The space between them was never filled – the Duke was beheaded on Tower Hill and no-one put his effigy there.

After Anglican worship ceased in this church it was let by the diocesan authorities to the Greek Orthodox community, which has now vacated the building.

It is hoped that St John Maddermarket will be preserved in entirety with its furnishings intact, and it has now been agreed that the Redundant Churches Fund (the national body funded by the Church Commissioners and the government) will take responsibility for it.

'There is a little chapel on the north enclosed by screens...'

St John de Sepulchre

THE church of St John de Sepulchre should really be known by its full dedication of St John Baptist and the Holy Sepulchre. It stands just inside the old city wall, a mere hundred yards from the gate through which travellers, having climbed up Bracondale, entered the long straight Ber Street on their way to the Castle and the city. Ber Street Gate was demolished in 1807 but fragments of masonry remain to show where it was – at a place where the wall had reached level ground after its climb from the river. Traditionally a street of butchers, of many pubs, of doubtful reputation, and much frequented by drovers and their cattle, Ber Street traverses the edge of a plateau which drops away steeply to the River Wensum on the east. On this side, where once were fields honeycombed with chalk workings, mid-nineteenth-century builders created a maze of narrow streets, squares and alleys filled with terrace cottage property.

Ber Street once had two other churches on its eastern side. Walking towards the city, one passes the stump of the tower of St Bartholomew's, a little church that was desecrated after the Reformation but whose fabric survived into the present century, when a part was in use as a tallow factory, and a cattle shed and slaughterhouse were built against its northern walls. Further along, one would have seen, until German bombs destroyed it, the church of St Michael at Thorn, standing among its hawthorn trees.

There is no mistaking the church of St John de Sepulchre, for its great tower, a city landmark, dominates the southern end of Ber Street. It is an aisleless church of flint with a small chancel, a two-storeyed north porch, and transepts on either side. The tower is reinforced by diagonal buttresses that step inwards at each of its four stages to reach a battlemented parapet with little pinnacles (added in 1904). It has tall Perpendicular belfry openings, a clock face with an eighteenth-century surround on the north, and a stair-turret on the south. The porch, through which one enters, is a pretty feature upon this somewhat sombre exterior – its surface enlivened by the use of flushwork among the flints.

Inside, the nave, lit by large windows on either side, is long and tall under a high-pitched roof; the windows are enclosed by deep wall arches, with hood-moulds and little half-columns over them. The small chancel is dimly

'...its great tower, a city landmark'

lit by three side windows, and an east window with stained glass in memory of the Reverend Samuel Stone, who died in 1848 and who, in his seven years as Vicar, became known as a great friend of the poor. The spiky-topped reredos confuses the window's subject and obscures its light. It was designed by John Oldrid Scott (and intended for another church); when it was erected in 1914 the Vicar hoped that it would provide an 'opportunity of cultivating taste in a poor parish'. The rest of the furnishings probably date from the restorations of 1866. Before that time there is mention of a Jacobean choir-and-organ gallery at the west end, a private pew belonging to Ber House over the north door, and a gallery in the north transept. The lower part of the chancel screen appears to belong to an earlier one, but it is impossible to accept any of the panel paintings as medieval. Those on the north side were 'carefully restored' by the Reverend Joseph John Gurney and the two on the south were presented by him.

Detail of lion font

Two memorial tablets in the chancel are interesting. One is to Bernard Church, Mayor of Norwich in 1651, who was a staunch Roundhead and a member of Cromwell's second parliament. The other is a very large memorial to the Watts family, erected by their 'last surviving relative', Mary Ann Watts, wife of Sir John Harrison Yallop. She seems to have been responsible for adding the lower and much larger portion of the monument to the simple sarcophagus above, which bears the name of James Watts (an 'eminent' butcher of 24 Ber Street).

In the nave is a fine East Anglian 'lion font', and on the wall are two sixteenth-century brasses, one reversed to show that the figure had been cut from brass previously used.

St John's is at present used by the Russian Orthodox community, which has made various changes in the furnishings to accommodate its style of worship.

Furnishings of the Russian Orthodox community

St John Timberhill

THIS church, anciently known as St John at the Castle Gates, and later as St John by the Timber Market, occupies a busy corner where Ber Street ends and Golden Ball Street and Timberhill begin; a place where the sound of lowing cattle from the market has given way to the noise of traffic. The Castle ceased to be a prison in 1887, and the nearby church of St Michael at Thorn has disappeared; it was in the churchyard there or in this at St John's that those who died in the gaol were buried.

The exterior of this little church is almost a complete rebuilding; the windows appear to be careful restorations, and the slated roof over nave and chancel with its little dormers, and the stone bell-turret at its western end, are unmistakably Victorian. There are remains of a priest's door below a window on the south and, at the east end, a few 'long and short' stones are visible in the chancel wall.

The man chiefly responsible for the church one sees today was the Reverend Edward Ram who, after three years as Curate at St Peter Mancroft, succeeded the Reverend Samuel Titlow as Vicar in 1871 and stayed for forty-seven years. St John's had long been neglected. In 1784 the square tower had fallen down and had been replaced by a little wooden bell-turret (Sillett's lithograph of 1828 shows a tiled chancel, and a thatched nave with this turret upon its gable). When Edward Ram arrived both porch and chancel were shored up with wood to prevent them from sharing the fate of the bell-turret which had already collapsed. Seven years later not only was the church in good repair but the Vicar was making such changes within that the Georgian interior was to disappear without trace.

Today, one enters a small, well-cared-for interior, much as conceived in the mind of Edward Ram a century ago. It has a short, wide nave, a short chancel with side chapels, three tall arcades opening from nave to aisles and another from the chancel into the south aisle, and a wooden barrel roof lit by two dormers. The walls and the tablets upon them, the piers, the font, the sword rests and one

'...three tall arcades opening from nave to aisles'

The font cover, made in 1929

brass candelabrum are all that remain of an earlier date.

Across the chancel entrance is an oak screen which supports a walk or rood loft, reached by a stone staircase in the wall. This screen is said to have come from Horstead church, which Phipson was restoring, and was put here in the 1890s, as was the rood beam with its crucifix and attendant figures (from Oberammergau). The south-eastern chapel was screened off about this time; here is a very good window and a recently painted altar frontal by Irene Ogden. Here, too, is a fine candelabrum with a figure of the Virgin among vine leaves (which Pevsner considers to be German of about 1500). Behind the altar is a large painted and gilded reredos of the triptych type, and before it hangs another fine candelabrum (this of about 1700). The figure of the Virgin with the Infant Jesus on the south of the chancel arch was sculptured by Martin Travers, a native of Norwich, and, in the 1920s, lecturer in stained glass at the Royal College of Art.

The organ, raised to allow passage under, and space for a small chapel, occupies the arch on the north of the chancel. The organ case, which faces down the aisle, has some excellent carving; the screen beneath was erected in memory of Edward Ram in 1920. The last piece of carved woodwork to be added to this pleasant and harmonious little interior seems to have been the font cover, made in 1929, from designs by E. J. Tench (and made, along with much of the other woodwork, by J. Howard and Sons).

St John's has one of the best wall tablets in Norwich, that on the wall of the chancel, where a cherub mourns the death of Robert Page (1778), the city's most famous 'statuary'. Much less distinguished is the memorial in the south aisle to James Cocksedge (Sheriff, 1827) and his sister. On the wall outside, as close as possible to their memorial, is a slab to Sarah Rackham, the family's faithful servant for more than fifty years. At the western end of the church the worn steps of the old north entrance now lead to a little vestry. There are sword and mace rests near the exit; under the large crown and the city arms are the names of John Angell (Mayor, 1830), and Arthur Michael Samuel (Lord Mayor in 1912–13).

St Julian

BLOMEFIELD had this to say of Dame (or Lady) Julian of Norwich who spent her life beside its walls so many centuries ago: 'In the east part of this churchyard stood an anchorage, in which an ankeress or recluse dwelt till the Dissolution, when the house was demolished, though the foundations may still be seen; in 1393 Lady Juliana, the ankeress here, was a strict recluse, and had two servants to attend her in her old age. This woman, in those days, was esteemed one of the greatest holiness.'

This tiny church, which has been almost entirely rebuilt after its destruction by bombs in the last war, stands on the hillside that slopes from Ber Street to King Street and the Wensum. John Chaplin was the architect for the postwar rebuilding of St Julian's, which was done very well. Its pre-Conquest tower which once stood so high above the church is now only a stump attached to a little nave where, on the north, some round Saxon win-

The fifteenth-century font

dows remain. The chancel, narrower and much lower, has, on the north side, a window with Decorated tracery and a priest's door. Within the pleasant churchyard one sees that the cast window has gone but that two small buildings have been attached to the southern wall, one over the south door and the other adjoining the chancel. That over the south door is a sacristy and the one on the east is a rebuilding of the cell of Dame Julian and contains her shrine. The interior has been skilfully rebuilt and all that remains of the original is perhaps the tomb slab (that Blomefield mentions as being here) to Charles Lulman, Rector of Postwick who died in 1697, and the slender fifteenth-century font at the west end. A pleasant painted and gilded reredos stands behind the altar; it has none of the spikiness of nineteenth-century examples. Within the tower is a pretty organ in a Gothic case (which looks early nineteenth century). The fine Norman doorway on the south came from the bombed church of St Michael at Thorn. Through this doorway one enters Dame Julian's cell, a quiet

Dame Julian's cell as rebuilt

little chapel with a window of stained glass that looks into the chancel.

The nineteenth-century history of St Julian's reflects the poverty of its surroundings, for this area, sandwiched between the breweries beside the river and the butcheries upon Ber Street, had been one of the city's worst slums. In 1827 Sillett made a drawing which showed the east window blocked up to the tracery, and a memorial tablet (of 1760) covering the southeast window. On 19 April 1845, the *Norfolk Chronicle* reported: 'On Monday morning last about eight o'clock the end of the chancel fell in and the noise greatly alarmed the neighbours.' That year William Mear rebuilt the east end (and inserted a mock Norman window), substituted slates for the chancel thatch, and repaired the ruinous tower. Other restorations followed in 1871 and 1901.

St Laurence

THE churches on the south side of St Andrew's Street and its westward extension, St Benedict's Street, stand high above the pavements, while those on the north are low, for the ground falls in that direction to the River Wensum. Street widening in the 1890s has left the church of St Laurence with a strip of churchyard along St Benedict's and none on Westwick Street, where it perches precariously on an eight-foot wall.

St Laurence's hides its size when viewed from St Benedict's Street, where its porch door is nine steps down from the pavement. But it is a very large church, similar in many ways to St Andrew's, and almost equal in size; the great clerestory has eleven windows and the tower is 112 feet high. In this church, too, there is no break between nave and chancel, and the roof runs continuously from end to end. St Laurence's also has two-storeyed porches on either side, but here they project from, and are not continuous with, the aisles. The completion date of the church is given as 1472 and the wide aisle windows, under shallow arches, are typical of the period.

Certain features of the great tower distinguish it from others in the city. It rises

'...the tower is 112 feet high'

by four stages and has the usual diagonal buttresses which reach the parapet, and large belfry openings. These openings have Decorated tracery and the battlements of the parapet are of the two-stepped kind, with tiny pinnacles at the angles. But it is the 'spirelet' over the stair-turret, a feature quite foreign to this area, that gives the tower its distinctive outline; it probably dates from a restoration of 1893.

Flights of steps at either end of the church lead down to Westwick Street, and from St Laurence's Little Steps beside the base of the tower one can inspect the frieze of shields at its foot and the details of the spandrels above the western door. The one on the left shows St Laurence being broiled to death on a gridiron at the command of the Emperor Decian; soldiers below replenish the fire while, from the sky, the Father Almighty strikes down the emperor with a sword. That on the right portrays the martyrdom of St Edmund, the Saxon king of East Anglia killed by the Danes in 869. Here, Danish soldiers aim at St Edmund, who stands bristling with arrows, and at the bottom corner, peeping from a cave among bushes, is the head of the wolf who guarded the saint's body.

Descending a little further, one can look along the tiny strip of burial ground set upon its high wall, where the handsome porch reaches almost to its edge. Westwick Street, overshadowed by the bulk of this great monument to fifteenth-century builders, presents the finest view of St Laurence's church. From this street one sees the full height of the tower, the same long clerestory as on the south, and the same large windows in an aisle which here is faced with stone and has a tiny vestry at its eastern end.

St Laurence's Steps take one back to the street above. They pass the large east window, rebuilt in Perpendicular style in 1894, when the old vestry which obscured it had been removed.

An air of desolation now pervades the interior of this magnificent church, once so flourishing but today dilapidated, stripped of its furnishings and with a floor which in parts is badly decayed. It is a great, spacious interior in which the high hammerbeam roof runs from end to end of the church. Wall posts from the roof descend between the windows of the continuous clerestory and rest on angel corbels; below them, tall arches open into wide aisles. A rood beam, deprived of its crucifix and attendant saints when the church was closed, crosses the nave and marks the entrance to the chancel; an opening in the southern pier shows that the pre-Reformation screen crossed nave and aisles at this point.

When the Reverend Edwin Hillyard became Rector in 1860 the church's latest acquisition seems to have been a west gallery of 1840, designed by Joseph Stannard and paid for by subscriptions from the parishioners. By the time the Rector had left in 1876, to become the Vicar of Christ Church, Belper, the gallery had been taken down, the high box-pews had been 'uprooted', a large rood screen erected and the altar raised on seven steps. (There are now more. Cautley mentions a crypt under the chancel and attributes the steps to this. An etching of 1838 by David Hodgson shows the interior of a crypt at St Laurence's.)

Edwin Hillyard was a pioneer of High Church practices in Norwich, and during his time the church became a centre of religious controversy. He had much to do with the Reverend Joseph Lyne, 'Father Ignatius' of the Elm Hill community, and in 1864 a number of his parishioners protested 'because the minister was allowing certain persons calling themselves monks to take a prominent part in the performance of the services'. The spiky fretwork screens across the aisles are now all that remains of Edwin Hillyard's rood screen.

Part of the south door

The pulpit (removed when the church was closed), reredos and rood beam are of much later date. The pulpit was made in 1917, and the reredos, dedicated as a war memorial in 1921, was constructed from the designs of Edwin Tench and includes painted panels by Kingston Rudd. The rood beam, with its crucifix and figures, was added in 1926 and was the gift of Martin Price Chamberlin, of the firm of Chamberlin and Smith. Records show that there was once much stained glass in the windows but that it was destroyed in 1643. There is little now, only a few old fragments in the north aisle, and a window of 1878 at the east end of the south aisle. This is to the Reverend John Crompton who succeeded Edwin Hillyard and who, despite the fact that he had for long been a dissenting minister of the French Church, was said on his arrival to have 'developed to the full the practices and ceremonies known as Ritualism.'

At the foot of the tower, where a door leads to the stair-turret, is the fine and unusual fifteenth-century font. This is octagonal and has quatrefoils upon the stem, while on the battlemented bowl angel heads appear above shields. There were some interesting brasses in the church on the walls at the west end and in the nave floor, but these were removed for safe custody when the church was closed for worship.

In the early 1980s there were grave fears that the church would collapse and the Sheriff (1983–4), Mr Norman Lake, started an appeal to save the church. This raised £25,000 which, together with additional funds contributed by Norwich Historic Churches Trust and English Heritage, has enabled adequate work to be carried out to preserve the church for the time being. However, many thousands of pounds will need to be spent before the building can achieve a secure future.

St Margaret

THREE churches stand very close together along the northern side of St Benedict's Street: on the east the big St Laurence's, on the west the small St Swithin's, and between them the medium-sized St Margaret's. From St Benedict's one sees St Margaret's as a grey building with walls of flint, with a slated nave roof, a chancel roof of tiles and an aisle that is roofed in lead. The aisle walls are pierced by very wide, shallow-arched Perpendicular windows; attached to aisle and tower is a two-storeyed porch with spandrels over its entrance arch. The tower appears broad at the base and narrow at the top, for its buttresses end at the belfry stage (where the belfry openings have Decorated tracery). On the north one sees the church through the trees of its large churchyard; here there is no aisle but a single-storey porch, a broad rood stair-turret, and a nineteenth-century vestry (on the wall of which an early carving of a crucifixion has been preserved).

Round this churchyard, as round so many others in the city, are those small signs that indicate by how many feet the churchyards have been reduced, and which show how narrow the surrounding streets must have been. There is nothing here to show by how much St Benedict's Street was widened, but on the west and north one discovers that St Margaret's and Westwick Streets were widened – the former by thirteen feet, the latter by seventeen feet, both at the expense of the churchyard.

To enter the church one steps down into the dark south porch, under the ribbed roof, and past the stone seats set along either wall. These seats are sad reminders of days when those who had to whip the dogs from the church had also to remove the destitute from the shelter of the porch before the service could begin.

The interior of the church – lit by the great windows on north and south – is bright on the dullest of days. The arches of the south arcade are very wide, the aisle is broad, and its windows are set in wall arches. The chancel is much narrower than the nave, and on the south a doorway communicates with the chapel of St Anne at the end of the aisle. The absence of an organ enables one to appreciate the proportions and details of this interesting little chapel. It is more a part of the chancel than of the aisle, for two arches open into it from the chancel, while access from the aisle is through a single, somewhat narrow opening. The pier beside this opening is pierced by an aperture which may have held a sanctus bell, or have been a 'squint' through which to view the altar. Three windows light the chapel, two on the south (one with a priest's door under) and one on the east, with a figure of St Margaret in stained glass (of 1966).

Upon the tomb chest below this east window there used to be a brass to Lady Anne Reed who died in 1567 (and whose husband has a brass in St Peter Mancroft), but this was removed when the church was closed for worship. On the wall are three excellent eighteenth-century tablets to members of the Brown family – wine merchants of St Margaret's parish. The adjoining chancel is raised by one step at the entrance and another at the altar, and has a door to the vestry on its northern side; the east window with its flame-like forms is by Michael King and was installed here in 1967.

The interior was changed in the nineteenth century in much the same way as were others in Norwich. From records one learns that in 1840 Joseph Stannard designed a gallery to stand before the tower arch. Then there was a period of neglect and disuse, then repairs in 1869, and finally restoration in 1886, when the gallery and old pews were removed, the church re-floored and a new vestry built.

For several years after its closure St Margaret's was used as a gymnasium, but this tenancy has now been surrendered, and Norwich Historic Churches Trust is seeking a new sympathetic use.

'... a grey building with walls of flint, with a slated nave roof, a chancel roof of tiles and an aisle that is roofed in lead'

St Martin at Oak

IT is surprising that so many of the small out-of-the-way churches of Norwich have managed to survive. One of these is the church with the curious name of St Martin at Oak, so called because of an oak tree that once stood in the churchyard, and in which, in the fifteenth century, was exhibited a much-venerated figure of the Virgin Mary.

This little church has survived the floods which over many centuries have visited the low-lying area of Coslany. It has stood its ground against the swarm of little houses that were built around it in the nineteenth century, and against the encroachments of the tall shoe factory that came in their place, and which shadowed the church's sunny side. Finally, after being bombed in the last war, and lying derelict until 1953, it has survived as St Martin's Hall. Across Oak Street another factory faces the church's western end. On the north all the old terrace houses have gone and left behind the ruined Pineapple pub where, in the paddock behind, Tom Hudson chopped wood and stabled his mare Rosie (in an atmosphere reminiscent of Cotman).

The surprise at the western end of the church is the former tower. This was never tall, but now, stripped of its top storey and provided with a stepped parapet on one face, it has become an elongated porch. The west end has several features which crowd together in delightful confusion. A narrow, square-headed window lights the aisle, and on either side is a stair-turret; one of these seems to have led into the tower and the other obviously provides access to the two-storeyed porch on the south. From here one can see that the building has no clerestory and a sweep of roof covers both nave and aisle.

On the north, only a narrow strip of ground separates the church from St Martin's Lane, for most of its churchyard was taken away in 1882. There is no aisle on this side; the nave has four Perpendicular windows with upright tracery and transoms. At the junction of nave and chancel is what appears to have been the rood stair-turret, now widened at its base, and with a door that gives entry to the chancel. The chancel is lower and narrower than the nave; it is roofed in slate and has two windows with Decorated tracery. A small, blocked-up window in the nave gable must once have opened above the chancel arch.

Those who rebuilt the little chancel in 1852 seem to have carefully preserved the features of the original. All the windows have Decorated tracery and are set in unusually deep wall arches. A small chapel extends southwards and may formerly have communicated with the aisle; it is lit by a small Perpendicular window. In it are several wall tablets, one in memory of Thomas Newton, a brewer, who was Mayor of the city in 1722. Another bears the name of Jeremiah Revans, who died in 1727, and of his wife, who died in 1711. Below the tablet, the large kneeling figures of Revans and his wife are perched upon a stone shelf. Blomefield describes the monument in his time, then complete and standing at the west end of the nave, where husband and wife knelt upon a large tomb and faced each other across a desk. He also tells us that Jeremiah Revans was Rector of East Tuddenham and, on his death, left a sum of money to assist in the education of six poor girls in St Martin's parish.

After repairs and redecoration St Martin's is now used as a night shelter for the homeless.

St Martin at Palace

THE Erpingham Gate, which gives entry to the Close from Tombland, was built by Sir Thomas Erpingham, that grand old knight, immortalised by Shakespeare in *Henry V*, who commanded the bowmen at Agincourt. From his house at the end of Palace Plain Sir Thomas must have seen the building of another beautiful gateway to the cathedral precincts, the one built by Bishop Alnwick, as the entrance to his palace. Palace Plain was then a part of the area known as the Liberty of the Prior, where the Prior had jurisdiction, both civil and criminal, over all who dwelt there. The Erpinghams may have seen, too, the building of the church upon the Plain, called St Martin at Palace, because of its closeness to the Palace Gate.

Much has happened in this corner of the city. It was here, in 1549, that Kett and his rebels, coming from Bishop Bridge, met and routed a company of Royalist troops and Italian mercenaries and slew their leader, Lord Sheffield. The Erpinghams no longer lived at the house at the end of the Plain; their place had been taken by another important family, the Calthorpes. Long after poor Kett had been hanged before the Castle and his brother on Wymondham tower – in quieter times two centuries later – the Calvinistic Methodists built a chapel upon a part of the grounds of Erpingham House. This building, which became the Countess of Huntingdon's Chapel in 1776, stood beside that charming old pub, the Adam and Eve.

Industry invaded the area in the nineteenth century and before its end the great gasworks building had spread over the site of Erpingham House. In 1882 it needed the combined opposition of the Dean and Chapter and the residents of the Close to defeat a scheme to make a railway across the Lower Close. Now the gasworks have gone and have been replaced by the splendid new buildings of the Crown and Magistrates' Courts.

The church is set upon a triangular churchyard where the road through the Plain divides, and can be described in much the same terms as many others in Norwich: with a western tower, a nave that is taller and narrower than the chancel, and a two-storeyed porch on the south. But it has clerestories (inserted in the second half of the nineteenth century) that differ from any of the others, for here light enters through three small quatrefoil lights on either side of the nave. The tower can be said to be different, too, for it has been rebuilt on at least two occasions. Had it been buttressed it might not have fallen, as its upper part did in 1783; then it seems to have been rebuilt without its top storey. During more restorations in 1874, it was raised to its original height by rebuilding the middle and top storeys.

The church is one of the earliest recorded in Norwich. According to Domesday Book it was held by Stigand, Archbishop of Canterbury, in 1066. The east wall of the chancel still retains long- and short-work dressings, a Saxon architectural technique. Excavations within the building by the Norfolk Archaeological Unit in 1988 revealed the footings of an Anglo-

The south porch and tower

Monument to Lady Elizabeth Calthorpe

The church is now used as a probation day centre

Norman church, occupying the same area as the present-day chancel and nave. These foundations for a stone building succeeded at least one, if not two timber precursors. Fragments of a decorated limestone graveslab could be dated to the tenth century, suggesting this date for the foundation of the church.

Through the porch one enters a short nave whose high roof receives little light from the tiny windows of the clerestory, one above each of the arches that open into the broad well-lit aisles. In the tall Perpendicular east window are three stained-glass figures on white surrounds which are signed as made by the firm of William Morris.

There is more stained glass at this end of the church. The south aisle has a window installed in 1861 to the memory of the Reverend Thomas Beckwith, and in the north aisle is a window with the arms of the Calthorpes, and the families with whom they were connected. The large monument below this window, a great stone table decorated with coloured shields, with an arched recess over it, is to Lady Elizabeth Calthorpe, who died in 1578. Her second husband was Sir Drue Drury, whose effigy kneels under a curtained canopy in the church at Riddlesworth in Suffolk.

Part of St Martin's collapsed in 1851, bringing down the north choir aisle and much of the chancel, except for the east wall. Until this sad event the north aisle contained two roundels of Norwich School stained glass, one depicting a sower and the other a reaper. Water-colour reproductions of these are held by Norwich Castle Museum.

After carrying out essential work to the tower and roofs, Norwich Historic Churches Trust has granted a lease to enable the church to be used as a probation day centre, its proximity to the courts and the probation office making it convenient for this purpose.

The alterations to the interior, to adapt the building to its new purpose, have been sympathetically designed by the firm of Peter Codling and present an attractive appearance with light airy structures enhancing the medieval character of the church.

St Mary Coslany

ON a city plan of 1886 one sees St Mary's parish as a network of narrow streets and courts, interspersed with malthouses, breweries and factories devoted to the manufacture of crape, hair, paper and cotton thread. It is a low-lying area where throughout the centuries the waters of the Wensum have been prone to rise in its narrow streets. One reads of floods from the sixteenth to the nineteenth century and how, in 1762, when the water was three feet deep in St Mary's church, many precious books and manuscripts were destroyed.

St Mary's stands upon a churchyard formerly much larger in the south, and then the largest in Norwich, at the junction of Pitt Street and St Mary's Plain. Its south side faces the widened Plain and looks across at the Baptist church which replaced an earlier one (of 1812) destroyed by bombs in the last war, to the charming thatched house once occupied by Thomas Pykerell, thrice Mayor of Norwich in the fifteenth century, and to the tiny Zoar Chapel which the Strict and Particular Baptists built next door in 1886. Its ancient fabric, built in 1477 against an Anglo-Saxon tower, has suffered greatly over the past hundred years.

It was restored between 1857 and 1869 but descriptions of its condition some forty years later make sorry reading. In the 1890s St Mary's parish is described as a 'region of noxious courts and alleys', and the church as in a state of 'extreme dilapidation'. By 1904 a large part of the tower had fallen down and a year later a newspaper correspondent described the building as being left to the mercy of 'stone-throwing street urchins', with piles of rubbish before its doors and the fabric incapable of restoration. But restored it was, for in 1908 the damaged portions of the tower were rebuilt, new windows inserted and the church put into a state of good repair. In 1942 the district was bombed and the roof reduced to a mass of charred timbers. Once again it was restored.

This grey flint church, with a porch of smooth stone, has an ancient round tower which must be the oldest of three such towers in Norwich, for its double belfry-openings with V-shaped heads and the recessed baluster-like shafts are unmistakably Anglo-Saxon. The church is cruciform, or cross-shaped, in plan, with nave, chancel and transepts, but without aisles. Its chancel is lower and narrower than the nave, and the windows, especially those in the chancel, are large, and all have Perpendicular tracery.

The south porch of smooth, pale, ashlar stone is a pretty addition to this church of dark flint. Above the entrance door is the usual niche with a window on either side to light the room within, and on the west side is a delightful turret.

Beyond the dark porch interior the long

The fine arch-braced roof

nave stretches eastwards to the chancel, flooded with light. A tablet to the Reverend Edward Thomas Daniell reminds one of other painters of the Norwich School who were associated with this church: John Sell Cotman who was baptised at this font in 1782, Crome who came here in 1792 to marry Phoebe Berney, and Robert Ladbrooke who was married here a year later. The arch-braced roof is very fine, especially where it meets the transept crossing, with its centre boss showing the Virgin surrounded by rays. One can see where the rood screen once stood across the chancel, for its stairs open out high on its northern wall and descend to a doorway in the transept. But perhaps it is the stained-glass windows in the north and south transepts that make the greatest impact upon the visitor. Both have handsome coats of arms. That in the north transept is in memory of Thomas Osborn Springfield, Mayor in 1829 and 1836, and Osborn Springfield, Mayor in 1863; that in the south transept is in memory of Peter Finch, Mayor in 1827.

The Springfield family controlled the firm of Springfield, Son and Nephew, well known in the last century as silk merchants in St Mary's parish, and Mayor Peter Finch was a member of the family of brewers in St Martin at Oak and the great grandson of the Reverend Peter Finch of the Octagon Chapel. The names of Mayors Springfield and Finch appear on the sword and mace rests, which are decorated with sprigs of leaves. There are several wall tablets of interest, notably one dated 1579, where the kneeling figures of Martin Van Kurnbeck, a doctor of medicine, and his wife are shown inscribed in stone. A comparison between the colourful tablet of 1753 to Alderman Hurnard, and that of 1828 to Martin Fountain, shows how the fashion changed.

Above the north porch is what appears to have been a little schoolroom. It is worth a visit if only to see the row of old-fashioned wooden hat pegs, or 'hat and cloak pins' as they were called in nineteenth-century school inventories. In this place, approached by winding stairs, low, dimly lit and incredibly small, one can picture some forgotten parson instructing his little class of factory children.

St Mary's is now the Norwich Craft and Design Centre and is open daily (except on Mondays) from 10 a.m. to 6 p.m. (Sundays until 4 p.m.).

St Mary the Less

ONE must look above the roof-tops in Queen Street to see the tower, or between the buildings to see the porch, for these are all that can be seen of St Mary the Less or, more commonly, the French Church. It has long been built around and against, and it hides itself from the passer-by. The church had a graveyard in Blomefield's time (1744), but even then it was enclosed by buildings for he says: 'There are houses built on the west, south, and east end of the church-yard, and the north part is a stone-cutter's yard.'

Today, two storeys of the grey flint tower rise above a shop building that is attached to its southern face. It is a tall, handsome tower, despite its bricked-in openings, the patchings of brick and stone upon its buttresses, and its encircling rods of iron. The buttresses are diagonal, and climb to a plain, flat parapet, above which is a weather-vane. Behind the buildings, the church stretches east towards Tombland, and double cast-iron gates mark its entrance upon Queen Street, where the porch is sandwiched between offices and shops. It is a plain porch with a gabled top, of two storeys, but with no window on the front, only the remains of a shallow niche. It leads into the dark interior of what was a small aisleless church, now stripped of its fittings. At the entrance two holy-water stoups are set back to back, one in the porch and one in the church; overhead an open wooden staircase ascends to the parvise. To the west is the narrow tower arch, as high as the ceiling of the nave; eastwards is the nave, whose windows have Decorated tracery, and the chancel, a little lower and narrower, with windows of a somewhat later style. The old north entrance is now filled by what looks like a house door, with plain glass in lurid Victorian colours.

The building has a long and curious history. It is said by various authorities to date from the thirteenth century, and to have borne the name of St Mary at the Monastery Gate. At the Dissolution, when it was no longer required as a place of worship, the Dean and Chapter leased it to Norwich Corporation in 1544, and soon after it was fitted up as a cloth hall where the newly arrived Dutch and Walloon 'strangers' were required to sell their cloth. They used the building until 1623, when it was made a hall for the sale of worsted yarn coming into the city; four years later the yarn men decided the place was too small, and ceased to use it. In 1637 St Mary's once again became a church, and began its long association with the French Protestants (hence the French Church) when the Walloon Company obtained a lease from the corporation, and undertook to repair and 'make fit the church of Little St Maryes to be used for God's worship'.

For nearly two centuries the French Protestants worshipped here, until in 1832 they leased it to the Swedenborgians, and the remains of the congregation gravitated to Unitarianism, and the Octagon Chapel. In 1857 Mrs Madders wrote: 'This congregation having by degrees fallen away and their language gradually ceased to be spoken by their descendants, at the suit of the heirs of the last deacon, P. M. Martineau Esq., trustees were appointed in Chancery to manage the estate, by whom it is leased to the Swedenborgians.'

The Swedenborgians seem to have used the church until 1869 when it was let to the followers of Edward Irving, the Scottish divine, who moved here from premises in Clement Court, Redwell Street. St Mary's became the Catholic Apostolic church, and so remained until 1953.

This new body made changes within the church – the *Norfolk Chronicle*, of 16 October 1869, records the removal of the old pews and west gallery, the raising of the sanctuary, the restoration of the parvise or chamber over the porch, and the construction of a staircase to it.

After being let for many years as a furniture store, the church has now been sold by the trustees, and a Dutch and Flemish studies centre may shortly be opened there, a happy revival of the link which this church had with the 'strangers' in the sixteenth century.

St Michael Coslany

A century ago the western end of Colegate must have been one of the busiest and noisiest parts of the city. Close by St Michael's (or St Miles') church were two ironworks and the great Anchor Brewery, with its maltings, smithies, and stabling for many horses. There is still much traffic in the streets that pass the church, but the noise of industry has left them. Now the trees that stood in the southern churchyard edge the pavement of a widened Colegate, and Oak Street is close to the western tower.

The exterior of St Michael's is impressive – a tall west tower, a nave without clerestory whose roof descends on to broad aisles lit by great wide windows, and a long, lower chancel. But what makes this church unique is the glorious display of flushwork upon the south aisle and parts of the chancel which Blyth, in 1842, likened to 'the inlaid ivory work of old cabinets'. The flushwork of aisle and chapel is original, but that upon the south and east walls of the chancel is a remarkably clever copy, the result of a restoration of 1883–4. This and more besides was carried out while the Reverend Sidney Selwyn was Rector. When he came to the church in 1881 he found a chancel of rough flints, whose east window had long been blocked up, and whose walls were unsafe; when he left in 1884 the chancel was as one sees it today. (The architect for the work was Edward Preston Willins, and the craftsman, W. Hubbard, of Dereham.)

The building of a porch and an adjoining aisle was begun by Alderman Gregory Clerk and completed by his son, another Gregory (Mayor of the city in 1505 and 1514). Its extension eastwards was made about the same time, by Robert Thorp, as a chapel to the Virgin Mary where, over his tomb, a chantry priest 'should sing perpetually for the sowl of Robert Thorp, his family, and al Christen sowls'.

On the north side is a plain flint aisle which was built by William Ramsey, a chandler, who was Mayor in 1502 and 1508.

The southern doorway gives entrance to the church; it is a poor little doorway which says

quite clearly that over it was once a porch. The nave is high and wide and looks into aisles that are brilliantly lit by great windows almost as wide as they are high, the vertical stonework of their tracery stiffened by cross-transoms, and each set within broad wall arches. Towards the east, beside the chancel arch, the position of the medieval screen is shown by the rood stair entrance and an aperture high up on the southern pier. Beyond is the chancel, which received the greatest attention at the time of the 1883-4 restorations, when the east window was inserted (with stained glass in memory of Richard and James Bullard).

It is probable that the east window was blocked up about 1740 to accommodate a very large classical reredos, described by several writers as being decorated with paintings by Heins. When the reredos was removed, the paintings found their way to Trowse church where they can be seen – the four Evangelists flanking the altar and a Resurrection on the south wall.

A joint building venture in the early 1980s, in which Norwich Historic Churches Trust restored the roof and main structure and Norwich City Council carried out internal alterations, means that the church is now a

The recently restored bellringing chamber

light and airy sports annexe to the adjacent Duke Street Centre. The city architect (A. C. Whitwood) has skilfully created a gallery at the west end, under which changing rooms have been tucked away.

The last step in bringing St Michael's back to a lively existence has been the restoration of the bellringing chamber so that the historic peal can again be heard in Coslany. This was effected by the Norwich Society, utilising a legacy contained in the will of Miss F. Foster.

The church is now a sports annexe to the adjacent Duke Street Centre

St Michael at Plea

SILLETT'S lithograph of St Michael at Plea, published in 1828, shows this church much the same as it is today, save that the tower is surmounted by a curious little cupola, and the porch has a large sundial over the entrance. These post-medieval features cannot have pleased later restorers, for the tower has since lost its cupola but gained four clumsy pinnacles, and the porch sundial has been replaced by the conventional niche. The tower is best seen from the bottom of St Andrew's Street, a view made possible in 1900, when St Andrew's was continued eastwards to meet Redwell Street to make a route convenient for trams. Until that time traffic bound from Bank Plain to St Andrew's Street had to go round via Princes Street, a tortuous and narrow way. (The road past the tower must have been incredibly narrow before 1884, for a notice says that, in that year, the wall was set back eight feet.)

Amid the grass of the raised churchyard, a beech tree droops over the great box-tomb of Sarah Allen, who died in 1809, and a slate slab upon a buttress commemorates one who spent his working life not far away – Robert Pitcher, 'for many years a respectable clerk in the banking house of Messrs R. B. and J. Gurney', who died in 1792.

The body of the church is of flint and has no aisles, while the fine two-storeyed porch is of light ashlar stone; in spandrels over the entrance are reliefs of St Michael and the Dragon. The nave has large Perpendicular windows set in somewhat sharply pointed arches. The heavy panelled door within the south porch opens into the tower and, through the western arch, one enters the interior.

The nave is high and light with a steep-pitched roof, along the ridge of which are angels holding shields. The western arch is tall, slender and beautiful, and across it a gallery, with Jacobean rails, leads to the parvise, or room over the porch. The fifteenth-century font stands on the north side of the nave – it is an octagonal font with a high seventeenth-century cover, supported on eight columns. Beside it, across an angle in the wall, is the oldest memorial in the church, that of Jacques de Hem (1603), which has a family group incised in the panel.

Looking to the east, and seeing the flimsy screen that was put across the chancel in 1907, one is reminded of its medieval predecessor, evidenced in the rood stair opening on the wall. This is the church which, until they were taken to the Cathedral, had one of the finest

The tower and newly restored porch

The church is now used as an exhibition centre

sets of fifteenth-century medieval screen paintings in the country.

The clock face of the tower bears the inscription 'Forget me not', a request which has not gone unnoticed during the past decade, for Norwich Historic Churches Trust has renewed the roof and repaired the main structure and a commercial sponsor has been responsible for restoration of the south porch.

The church is now in use as an exhibition centre under commercial management, after a skilful conversion which has placed lavatories and kitchens unobtrusively in the south transept, the architect being Michael Gooch.

Octagon Chapel

THE nineteenth century saw the deterioration of Colegate from a street of gentlemen's houses to one devoted to industry. When did the change begin: when the ironworks arrived at its western end, or with the timber yards further east? In the eighteenth century, when the city's textile industry was most prosperous, several wealthy textile manufacturers lived there; good dwellings faced the street, many with their gardens and carriage houses behind. Robert Harvey, 'father of the city' in 1738, lived then at No. 20; No. 18 was the home of Thomas Harvey, Mayor in 1748, and there, too, lived his son Jeremiah Ives Harvey when Mayor in 1783. The Ives family lived in Colegate in the same century, Amelia Opie was born there, and even old Bacon House became a mayoral residence again when William Wiggett took office in 1742.

It was into this Georgian street that the Octagon Chapel came in 1756 – a building eminently suited to its surroundings. The Presbyterians, whose chapel it was, had had a place of worship on a part of this site since 1687, hidden away from Colegate and approached by a passage from Calvert Street. Now, almost a hundred years later, the great carriage gates of their new meeting house could open proudly upon Colegate (its Congregational neighbour of 1693 hence becoming 'the Old Meeting House'). Early last century the congregation became identified with Unitarianism, and the building became known as the Octagon Chapel.

The architect of this remarkable building was Thomas Ivory, whose drawings had been chosen from a number submitted to the church committee (and which included designs by Robert Brettingham and Thomas Rawlins). Ivory, who was busy with the building of the Assembly House, did what many other architects have done before and since – he took his inspiration from the work of another man. This was James Gibbs, architect of St Mary le Strand in London and the Radcliffe Camera in Oxford, who in 1728 had published a book of his own works, which included the rejected design for a circular church of St Martin in the

Fields. There is no doubt that the Octagon is a simplified adaptation of this Gibbs design. Norwich was fortunate that it had, in Thomas Ivory, one who could do it so skilfully and successfully.

The chapel itself is little changed since John Wesley described it in 1787 as 'eight square, built of the finest brick, with sixteen sash windows below and as many above'. These windows, unlike those of the Old Meeting House, are recessed to conform with the fire prevention statute of 1709.

Of the interior, Wesley wrote: 'The inside is furnished in the highest taste and is as clean as any gentleman's saloon.' The portico provides a foretaste of what is within, for the Octagon's simple external skin of brick conceals an elegant interior. Through a small vestibule, one enters the chapel where a ring of giant Corinthian columns soar towards the ceiling, linked at their centres by the galleries, and above by great semicircular arches. Overhead is a curving panelled ceiling, pierced by little circles of light. Below, rows of pews fill the centre of the auditorium and rise in tiers beneath and upon the galleries. The changes made to the pulpit and organ between 1887 and 1889 are obvious to those who have visited the Old Meeting House. The dignified little pulpit was extended on either side to form a railed rostrum, the organ doubled in size, the high box-pews lowered, and additional doors made into the vestibule.

The wall tablets vary from pretty eighteenth-century ones in coloured marbles to the duller memorials of the next century. The best are those to the Reverend William Enfield (1759) by John Athow, and to Sarah Petty, wife of a silk throwster (1751) by Thomas Rawlins. The tablet to the surgeon Philip Meadows Martineau, who died in 1829, reminds one of his fine house which stood on the site of County Hall. The rather plain sword and mace rests show the names of four mayors and one Lord Mayor of 1953 – the writer Ralph Mottram, whose ancestors worshipped here since 1689.

A door into the vestry leads into a small graveyard on the western side; it is a quiet place overlooked by the back of that fascinating little terrace called Pope's Buildings, and by a large house, now gone over to commerce.

Old Meeting House

READING of the rise of Nonconformity in Norwich, one of the first names one encounters is that of the Reverend William Bridge – Rector of St Peter Hungate and Curate of St George Tombland – who about 1635 fled to Holland to join the Independent Church in Rotterdam. He and others had refused to conform to the 'popish ceremonies and divers innovated customs' of Bishop Wren of Norwich (father of Sir Christopher). They did not return to this country until 1642 when they founded an Independent church in Yarmouth, with Mr Bridge as their Pastor. Five years later they established another church in Norwich (Blyth says that their services were held, until 1640, in a brewhouse in St Edmund's), but they had no permanent home until they built the Old Meeting House in 1693.

One must search to find this modest building, which stands at the end of an alley off Colegate. This, its only approach, had an ornate cast-iron archway over the entrance – now there is nothing to tell you that this narrow way leads to one of the earliest and finest meeting houses in the country. Beyond the entrance gates and a little forecourt is its southern front, a gracious symmetrical façade of red brick, divided into five bays by giant pilasters with Corinthian capitals of Portland stone. Two rows of sash windows, said to be the earliest in Norwich, light the interior, plain hooded doorways are at either end, and there is a painted sundial between the middle windows. It is a building without show, a rectangular brick box with a roof of dark tiles, which achieves its quiet dignity by good proportion. This is the style that was to set a

standard of tasteful building for the next hundred years.

The Old Meeting House has little ground to call its own, and even its approach is now inhabited by cars. Its forecourt, formerly a burial ground, was made smaller when the Sunday School was built in 1842 (which spoils one's view of the façade), and again about 1930, when the little Neill Room was added. Until recent years, the garden of St Clement's Rectory stretched beside the graveyard, behind the meeting house. The garden has now become a car park and the peace of the place has gone. One must be thankful for the presence of the two Georgian houses, one in red brick and one in grey, that overlook its northern side.

The interior seems to have changed little since the day it was opened. A narrow vestibule stretches between the entrance doors, and there are doors to the galleries and ground floor. Beyond is the church, a simple auditorium, a place of dark wood with walls of sober cream. A tall pulpit, with elegant staircases, occupies the centre and looks down upon curving rows of pews, and up to galleries which encircle the three remaining walls; these stand upon Tuscan columns, and above them columns with Ionic capitals and quaint bits of entablature stretch to the ceiling.

On the western gallery is an organ with gilt pipes and a pretty carved case, and from the south gallery a large octagonal clock face looks towards the pulpit. On either side of the pulpit two black grave-slabs have been reared upon the wall; one from an earlier church is to John Coney (1658), and the other to John Lucas, who died in 1703. By contrast the tablet over the pulpit, with its white sarcophagus on a black oval, shines out like a little jewel. It is in memory of the Reverend Samuel Newton (d. 1810) and was carved by an almost unknown Norwich sculptor, Joshua Cushing. On the same wall are two tablets by John Ivory: they commemorate the Reverend Thomas Scott (1746) and John Dawson (1721).

Other memorials are under and above the galleries: to Jeremiah Tomson (1721), 'a great admirer of Free Grace'; to Thomas Theobald, maker of dyes who is described as 'one of the principal manufacturers'; and to John Jarrold, founder of the printing firm, who died in 1852.

In 1970 it was realised that repairs to the fabric were urgently needed and the work was carried out by the city council, because it was realised that the cost was completely beyond the resources of the reduced congregation. The Old Meeting House continues to be used occasionally for services.

The Jarrold memorial

St Peter Hungate

LIKE its neighbour St Simon and St Jude, at the foot of Elm Hill, the church of St Peter Hungate was saved by being put to other uses, and is now a well-kept, well-warmed, and very exciting museum of church art. Elm Hill drops steeply beside its tower with the curious slate hat – a tower so low that the churchyard tree overshadows it. From here the church's southern side lies along Princes Street.

First one sees the stair-turret to the parvise, in the angle between the tower and the two-storeyed porch, where in the niche above the entrance one may, in spring, see a blackbird upon her nest. This is the porch said to have been built by Nicholas Ingham, a mercer, who was buried in it in 1497. Beyond is the nave with Perpendicular windows so tall that they almost reach the eaves; then there is the transept with even larger windows, and finally the chancel, a little lower and with wide Perpendicular windows. The nave and transept roofs are of lead and low in pitch; that of the chancel is steeper pitched and of tiles.

The churchyard is narrow along Princes Street, and non-existent where Elm Hill passes the tower, both streets having been widened in 1907. Round on the east a row of flint and brick cottages overlooks the churchyard, and a smaller window, set high in the wall of the church, lights the chancel. On the north, the square churchyard slopes downwards, not as steeply as Elm Hill, to where the fifteenth-century Briton's Arms is built against it. The features of the church are much the same as on the south: large Perpendicular windows in the nave and transept, windows a little smaller in the chancel, and a north door but no porch. A little vestry that Sillett showed (in a monochrome of 1828) as attached between the two chancel windows has gone, but the rood stair-turret remains in the angle between chancel and transept.

'...a well kept, well warmed, and very exciting museum of church art'

Blomefield states that John Paston and his wife Margaret (whose house on Elm Hill is now the Strangers' Club) secured the patronage of the old St Peter's church from the College of St Mary in the Fields in 1458 and rebuilt it 'as a neat building of black flint'. On a buttress near the north door appears the date of its completion (1460) together with a tree trunk without branches, which symbolises the decay of the old church, and a branch springing from the root, which denotes the new one.

Returning to the south, one steps down into the porch and, through it, enters a light aisleless nave of splendid proportions. On either side the broad Perpendicular windows, set in deep wall arches, reach up to the roof – a beautiful and unusual roof, of low pitch, heavy-beam construction, where angels holding books and scrolls look down into the nave. In front of the entrance to the tower is the sturdy fifteenth-century font with a small, seventeenth-century cover. One tablet remains on the west wall, a very good one to Matthew Goss, a dyer and 'an inhabitant of this parish for sixty years' who died in 1779. (Monastery Court was formerly Goss's Yard and this gentleman lived in the house that stood across its entrance.) The floors are paved with square Norfolk tiles, except where the memorial slabs, that once lay between the pews, stretch down the centre of the nave and up into the chancel. There are many things to discover within this church – the blocked-up openings to the rood-screen stairs, the 'squints' in the transept piers, the stoup beside the north door, the Royal Arms over the south door, and much more.

For the visitor who wishes to learn its history and the meaning of the things to be found here, there is an excellent booklet by Rachel Young and Geoffrey Goreham, which is on sale at the museum stall. From it one can obtain a picture of this small parish throughout the centuries: how the Sack Friars came in the thirteenth century, and were later ousted by the Black Friars; how in the nineteenth century the self-styled Father Ignatius (the Reverend Joseph Leycester Lyne) tried to form a religious community in Elm Hill; and, finally, how its church became a city museum in 1936.

St Peter Mancroft

NORWICH has one of the most attractive open markets in the country. Blomefield, about 1744, called it 'the grandest Market, as well as the best single market in all England'. The Castle Museum has a remarkable collection of paintings and prints which convey better than many words what the Market Place was like in the nineteenth century. They show an area of stalls that is wider on the north where it sprawls across the Guildhall, but narrower towards the west where the buildings come down level with the Guildhall's eastern end. On three sides gable-fronted buildings stand cheek-by-jowl with dignified Georgian façades, and they look down upon a place crowded with stalls and busy with people. An early picture shows a market-cross amongst the stalls, a later picture shows the statue of the Duke of Wellington, and later still there stands the first gas-lamp to be seen anywhere in Norwich.

The pictures show that everywhere, among the fringe of buildings, there were pubs. They stand against the churchyard of St Peter Mancroft, which is ringed round with buildings. They are on the west, and on the east; along Gentleman's Walk are larger ones, coaching inns, some with yards that stretch through to the Back of the Inns, beside Castle Ditches.

Alderman Davey was responsible for one of these inn yards becoming Davey Place when the King's Head was demolished in 1812. Another, the yard of the Royal, was transformed into the Royal Arcade (by George Skipper) at the beginning of this century. The Royal was formerly the Angel, well known as the headquarters of the 'Blue and White' or Whig Party; in 1846 it was given a new name and a new front by the architect, Joseph Stannard. (This front still stands although shorn of its cornice and coat of arms.)

The church of St Peter Mancroft, or St Peter and St Paul at Mancroft, is the largest in the city and is often mistaken by visitors for the Cathedral. The ground on which it stands slopes to the east, so that its eastern end is high above Weavers' Lane, where there is the dark building which houses the sacristy.

Its great tower is up beside St Peter's Street and its northern side faces the market. One great unbroken roof covers nave and chancel, and below it run the ranges of seventeen clerestory windows on north and south. Lower down are tall aisles, each with a projecting porch and a shallow transept, and at ground level are bands of flushwork and shields.

St Peter's was built in the Perpendicular style between 1430 and 1455 on the site of a church which was under the patronage of the Abbey of Gloucester. Perhaps this early

'...a multitude of canopied niches and shallow panels'

association with Gloucester may account for the fact that its tower is like no other in Norwich. Massive and of great height, it hides its features under a multitude of canopied niches and shallow panels, which crowd upon each face. Its topmost stage was restored in accordance with the designs of George Edmund Street and his son, A. E. Street, and the work carried out between 1881 and 1895 (in the latter year the flèche, made by John Downing and Sons of Victoria Street, Norwich, was erected).

In 1882 the churchyard was lowered, houses removed from within its eastern and southern boundaries, and the railings and pepper-castor gateposts added. The front of the fine two-storeyed north porch was restored in 1904 (by the architects Bucknell and Comper).

Before entering the church one might pause to read the inscriptions on the tomb that stands near the porch. R. H. Mottram, in his book *The Speaking Likeness*, explains why the name of a young actress appears there along with those of two mayors and their families. He tells of Sir John Harrison Yallop's love for Sophia Ann Goddard, who died of consumption in 1801 when only twenty-five, and who, after her appearances at the Theatre Royal, was said by the Norwich Mercury to 'lose nothing by comparison with Mrs Siddons'.

Through the porch one enters an interior of quite staggering size, one where no chancel arch breaks the vista eastwards and the eight bays of the aisle arcade march from end to end. Looking at this elegant arcade, one wonders that such slender piers, so tall and widely spaced, can support those great arches, with their wall above, and, crowning all, the heavy hammer-beam roof, which is topped with lead.

At the west the tower arch rises as high as the ridge, and on either side the windows of the aisles and clerestories flood the place with light. The east end glows with colour, from the great east window, upon the gilded reredos, and in the windows of the chapels of St Anne on the south, and of Jesus on the north.

The furnishings are Gothic, Victorian, and very good. Most were put there during the thirty years that the Reverend Charles Turner was Vicar. In 1851 Phipson took charge of restorations that in five years seem to have resulted in the removal of every Georgian feature from the interior.

This short, sharp 'battle of the styles' seems to have ended here, but it is interesting to note that two of the vanished Georgian features returned to the church. One is the handsome classical case which encloses the east-end organ in the south aisle, once a part of the organ loft that stood before the western arch, bearing the date 1707. It was brought back in 1911 through the efforts of Wallace King, then a churchwarden, who discovered it in a country house. For the clock face was substituted a portrait of the daughter of the Vicar, the Reverend Frederick Meyrick, by his father-in-law, Sir William Richmond.

Another piece of work that returned can be found in the sacristy, for the top of a large table there is none other than the sounding-board of the pulpit 'of the time of Charles I' (a brass plate says that it was presented by P. E. Back in 1893).

The present reredos behind the high altar is the one erected in 1886 (made by Harry Hems in Exeter, and designed by John Pollard Seddon), to which the lower figures were added (including the oriental-looking Christ in Glory), and the whole coloured and gilded under Sir Ninian Comper's direction in 1930.

'...an interior of quite staggering size'

The great east window

Two bays short of the eastern walls of the aisles, a step takes one up into the chancel at the point where the medieval rood screen crossed the church, for the entrances to it can be seen high up on the north and south walls. Each has a door below, which opens on to winding stairs; on the north the stairs continue downwards to a crypt below the Jesus chapel, which long ago became the burial vault of the Back family.

The great east window is the church's finest feature. Its forty-two panels illustrate stories of Christ, the Virgin, St John the Evangelist, and others. One of the donors, Thomas Elys (or Ellis), three times Mayor of Norwich in the fifteenth century, appears in one panel, and in others are members of the Garnish and Ramsey families. The central strips and single panels on either side of the base are nineteenth-century restorations. The east window, together with all the others in the church, was blown out during the Civil War when a powder magazine exploded in Bethel Street. Eventually enough of the medieval glass was collected to fill the east window, although not all the panels were restored in their original form. Nevertheless the glass in this great window remains some of the finest in the country.

There is good later stained glass in the church: to Robert Seaman (1874); to Archd. William Pelham Burn (1902), who died on a Tyrolean holiday; to the sisters of Thomas Gillett of Boyton House, Ipswich Road (1911); and to those who died in the 1914–18 War (by H. Hendrie).

A brass beside the sanctuary steps commemorates Sir Peter Rede (1568), who was knighted by the Emperor Charles V. It seems to have done duty for an earlier knight, for his armour is a century out of date.

Two wall tablets face each other across the chancel: one to Dorothy, wife of the great Sir Thomas Browne (1685), and the other to Sir Thomas himself (1682). Below his tablet is one to Mary Bowman, and it was during the digging of her grave in 1840 that the coffin of Sir Thomas was discovered. The skull was removed and found its way to the Norfolk and Norwich Hospital; there it remained until

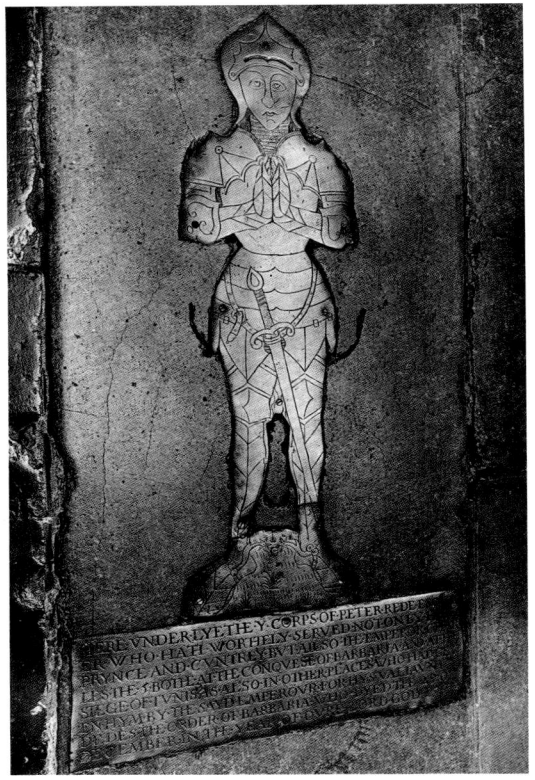

A brass commemorating Sir Peter Rede

Memorial tablet to Sir Thomas Browne

1922 when it was reinterred below his memorial.

The south transept, which until recently was filled with organ pipes, has now been skilfully restored as The Chapel of the Blessed Virgin Mary for private devotions. St Nicholas' Chapel in the north transept now houses the Mancroft Heritage Exhibition. Here many treasures of the church are on permanent display. They include a twelfth-century illuminated manuscript, a Vulgate bible in Latin, an alabaster panel representing nine female saints, several paintings and a magnificent collection of plate. Pride of place must go to the Gleane Cup, made in 1565 and presented to the church in 1633 by Sir Peter Gleane, a former Mayor of Norwich.

The large wooden canopy over the font is a rare feature; there are only three others in the country. Although the supporting posts are original, the canopy is a Victorian reconstruction, the original having been destroyed by Cromwellian troops. The font is a 'seven sacrament font' which had paintings of the seven sacraments – christening, confirmation, Holy Communion, marriage, ordination, anointing the sick and absolution – on the side panels. The eighth panel had the *rose en soleil*, the badge of Edward V.

On the walls of the tower's ringing chamber are boards recording feats of teams of ringers. One, the oldest peal board in the country, tells how in 1715 the first true peals of 5,040 changes were rung 'and not one bell misplaced'. There are thirteen bells in the tower, twelve of which are regularly rung.

In 1979 an appeal was launched by the church to provide funds for repair and restoration of the fabric, for a new organ and to provide ancillary facilities, including the 'Octagon', an eight-sided meeting room built onto the south-east corner of the church. In all some £425,000 was raised and the work is now complete.

The Collins organ, which was installed at the west end in 1984 at a cost of £120,000, is one of the finest instruments of its kind in the world. It is a reproduction of an eighteenth-century north-German baroque organ with a strikingly designed modern case.

St Peter Parmentergate

ON its large churchyard that drops steeply down to King Street stands the church of St Peter. It boasts two names – St Peter Parmentergate and St Peter Permountergate, the former more commonly used. The churchyard is full of fine trees, and one should spend a little time here before entering the church. The east end, with its two-storeyed vestry at its foot, is so high above King Street that ten steps are required to reach the priest's door in the chancel.

The windows of nave and chancel are tall and Perpendicular in style with deep-stepped buttresses between. The south porch, which is two storeyed and attached to the aisleless nave, has spandrels over the door, a square-headed window above, and a plain gable above that. Beside it is the large box-tomb of Robert Martin, Sheriff's Officer, who died in 1868. The western tower is very fine, with battlements, tall Perpendicular belfry windows, square sound-openings and a handsome western door. Beyond the tower the churchyard still climbs steeply and ends at a twelve-foot wall in which are the vaults of the Aldred family of 1800–50. From this point the church can be seen to advantage – its walls and tower of flint, the nave taller than the chancel and roofed with slate, the chancel roofed with tiles. The north side shows that the church once had a north entrance, and here are two stair-turrets, one against the tower, and another, which led to the rood screen, curiously embedded into an aisle window.

Entering the church and looking down the nave, one is impressed by its loftiness and by the beauty of the wide chancel arch. The nave roof is of medium pitch and the later chancel roof is high pitched. The chancel floor has been raised and one ascends six steps from chancel entrance to altar. Across this entrance is the lower part of a fine fifteenth-century carved screen, of which Cautley and others state that the north side is original and that on the south an exceedingly good copy. The east window, placed high to look over the vestry, is filled with strongly coloured Victorian glass.

On the north side of the chancel arch can be seen the entrance to the rood stairs and up against the eastern wall is the highly coloured reredos erected in 1890 by the Reverend William Hudson in memory of his wife.

The finest thing in the chancel is the monument to Richard Berney and his wife Elizabeth, whose family built a large house near the church of St Martin at Palace, and later had a house in King Street. Their praying figures lie, rather stiffly, under a great four-poster canopy, which is decorated with strapwork, a bold coat of arms, and the usual symbols of Jacobean funeral sculpture. The monument was erected in 1623 by Elizabeth Berney's father, Edward Hobart, of Hales Hall, for she had wished to be buried in the chancel of this church and 'for a decent memorial tomb to be placed there'.

The font, at the west end, is a good example of the fifteenth-century East Anglian type. It is octagonal, with lions and angels holding shields upon the bowl, and human heads and heads of beasts below it. On the shaft are those mysterious 'wild men' holding clubs and shields, and between them little buttresses.

Full restoration of the tower and main structure has recently been completed by Norwich Historic Churches Trust and negotiations are proceeding for converting the church into a museum.

St Saviour

IN the early nineteenth century when St Saviour's had a thatched roof it must have looked even more rustic than it does now. Even today it looks much like a village church that has come to town. Short and low, it squats upon a small churchyard, with a stumpy tower that rises only a little above the roof of the nave, and stands only a few feet from the pavement. The nave, much wider than the tower, has more roof than wall and is without aisles or clerestory. The chancel is earlier, being fourteenth century, and is a good deal lower and narrower than the nave. Whether the tower was ever any higher is open to conjecture; the sound-hole on the western face suggests that it was, and the parapet has obviously been rebuilt. The east end is charming – here under a steep gable is a beautiful Decorated window whose tracery is enriched with cuspings, and beside it a small but very pretty eighteenth-century tablet, with carved hanging drapery.

Here, as elsewhere round the church, the pale tombstones have been removed from the once larger churchyard, and cluster at the foot of the wall. On one, above the name Henry Peace Silcock and the date 1816, a forge and anvil stand under a weeping tree. On the south is a humble porch which, after being used as a baptistry for a century, was reopened in 1891. The Gothic gallery which once spanned the western end, and which was supported on two cast-iron columns, can now be seen in All Saints', Westlegate. Probably this gallery was where the choir was seated, for a notice once there stated 'Boys must come to church clean and tidy and must be quiet, reverent and orderly in church'!

The nave has a curved plaster ceiling, crossed by heavy tie-beams which look suspiciously Victorian. Similar tie-beams were removed from the chancel in 1923, when the roof was rebuilt. Here, Commandment boards of metal are still upon the east wall.

In the chancel is some oak panelling erected in memory of the Reverend Harris Cooke, who was Vicar here for fifty-three years. Mr Cooke, a parson of the old school, came four years after the restorations of 1852, and must have kept the interior much as he found it. He it was who in 1864 repelled an invasion of the church by the monks of Father Ignatius, who had caused so much dissension at St Laurence's.

No-one who visits St Saviour's should leave the district without taking a good look at Magdalen Street. The present street is so busy and so full of traffic that only on Sundays can one recognise it for what it was – a street of town houses interspersed with smaller dwellings. Eminent men and women have lived here: Sir William Hooker, the botanist, the Gurneys, Harriet Martineau, and Elizabeth Fry, to name but a few. The finest

building in the street is the great Georgian house that stands opposite the church (which Pevsner suggests was built between 1740 and 1750). Its dignified façade is structurally linked with its neighbour, which was undoubtedly built, perhaps a little later, to accommodate the delightful Georgian shop at street level. The house is said to have been bought by Richard Smith in 1809, his son Joseph opening the shop next door at about the same time, as the second druggist's establishment in the city.

When St Saviour's was declared redundant the furnishings were removed and the building is now used as a badminton hall.

St Simon and St Jude

ELM Hill is an example of what can be done in preserving, not single buildings, but a whole street. That it was saved is greatly due to the efforts of a few enthusiasts who nearly seventy years ago formed the Norwich Society, one of whose first concerns was with the preservation of this little street. In those days Elm Hill seemed hardly worth preserving, and the corporation had decided that it was to go. The place had become little better than a slum and many of its fine old houses were very dilapidated. They had long been hemmed in behind by a multitude of properties, little factories that had become dwellings and houses that had become workshops. In the 1850s Mrs Madders wrote: 'Messrs Towler and Company's shawl factory is upon Elm Hill', and Bayne mentioned a firm named Wright and Son as having a factory there which made ' plain and fancy fabrics' and formerly employed 1,500 hand-loom weavers. Both have left their names upon courts in the street .

The Norwich Society's campaign to save Elm Hill was protracted but successful, as were its protests against the proposal to demolish the church of St Simon and St Jude, the small church which stands where the hill meets

The churchyard on the south – a secluded place overlooked by a blank wall

'He kneels in mayor's robes, facing his wife Christian'

wealthy gentlemen were either causing damage to, or being damaged by, the churchyard wall, for in 1747 ex-Mayor Robert Harvey was given leave to set the wall back by three feet, because of the damage caused by carriages.

For a century the story of this little church was one of almost continuous neglect. It was closed in 1892, and five years later was in such bad repair that the church authorities decided to let it become a ruin. What happened in the next few years is not clear, but one learns that in 1913 the Reverend W. F. Crewe renovated the interior and used it as a Sunday School until his death in 1920. Again the church was closed, and photographs show it, a few years later, completely enveloped in ivy. In 1940 it was repaired by the Norwich Amenities Society, and twelve years later it was adopted by the Norwich Boy Scouts Association.

The famous Pettus monuments are still against the walls, on either side of the chancel arch, boxed in to protect them from damage. The one on the south is the earlier, that to Thomas, who was Mayor in 1590 and lived in Pettus House, a part of which remains on Elm Hill. He kneels in mayor's robes, facing his wife Christian, across a prayer desk, and their family kneel behind them. On the north is a much larger tomb of Sir John Pettus, Mayor in 1608, who moved from Elm Hill to an estate at Rackheath. Sir John, in armour, lies uncomfortably on his elbow, and the hand beneath his face holds a glove. Above him are two of his sons and four of his daughters, and higher still, kneeling in a recessed arch, are his son, Sir Augustine Pettus, and his wife Abigail. (Sir Augustine died a year before his father, in 1613.)

Wensum Street. It is a building of great antiquity which is said to have been held by the bishops before the see was removed to Norwich. This is a simple flint church, with neither aisles nor porches, a chancel which (by its windows) is older than the nave, and a ruined tower (partially demolished in 1911). Perhaps its most unusual feature is its east window upon Wensum Street, not high but very broad, with wide-spaced mullions that curve in its upper part to enclose large ogee-shaped areas of glass.

The only churchyard it can be said to possess is that on the south, a secluded place now overlooked by a blank wall where in the 1880s Edward Willins drew a row of gabled houses which he noted as being 'in a ruinous state of decay'. The rest of its burial ground has been reduced to a narrow strip along Elm Hill, and a fragment on the east beside Wensum Street. St Simon's must once have stood upon an ample churchyard, for one reads that in 1492 a man named John Eastgate had taken sanctuary there and that the city burgesses were to be paid 'any costs or expenses for ye taking of John Eastgate out of sanctuary'. By the eighteenth century the narrowness of Wensum Street opposite the Maid's Head was hindering the passage of traffic. The carriages of certain

'...lies uncomfortably on his elbow'

St Stephen

THE tower of St Stephen's, best seen from Rampant Horse Street, is unique. No other Norwich church has one that is, in effect, a three-storeyed porch attached to the north aisle, nor has any other tower such a wealth of pattern upon its surface. This pattern, which increases in richness from the ground up, is one of colour contrasts and not, as on St Peter Mancroft tower, a pattern of light and shadow. Above the entrance is a band of light shields among the flints, then two bands, and finally a glittering top storey of white stone, where flints are used only as flushwork inserts into two dummy windows and three geometrical shapes. There are no battlements, only a low capping surmounted by a weather-vane. It is most certainly not the grandest church tower in Norwich, but it is the prettiest. The large numerals over the doorway which gave the date 1601, and probably referred to an early restoration, have unfortunately been removed.

On this north side the aisle stretches the full length of the church and is intersected by a transept. Aisle and transept are of flint with large Perpendicular windows and are roofed, like the nave, with lead. The beautiful clerestory is clothed in smooth stone, its sixteen close-set windows being separated by most delicate buttresses similar to those on the topmost storey of the tower. On the south side is the same unbroken line of clerestory windows set in the same smooth stone. There is no transept on this side, and the flint-faced aisle stops short of the eastern end of the church, to allow for a single-storeyed vestry. The south entrance, with its arch in the Decorated style, seems to have had a projecting porch, and there is a priest's door further east.

The eastern and western ends of the church are fascinating, yet puzzling – though obvious restorations, they are very fine indeed. Both ends are faced in white stone and in the western one, set between deep, stepped buttresses, and above a doorway of moderate size, is a great window whose upper part, filled with vertical tracery, rises as high as the windows of the clerestory. The many pieces of masonry still lying in the churchyard are evidence of considerable rebuilding; indeed, a pleasant little seat surround has been made from fragments of pinnacles, and the original of an inscribed slab which appears between the west door and window with the date 1550. The east end is taller because of the slope of the ground, and it, too, has a very large Perpendicular window, set high to shed light above the reredos within. The church was restored both inside and out by R. M. Phipson during the

'...set between deep, stepped buttresses, and above a doorway of moderate size, is a great window'

The window in the north transept

incumbency of the Reverend Edward Evans-Lombe; the date of the work appears at the base of a curious detached pinnacle (a cupola on the west gable was taken down in 1789).

The ground floor of the tower, through which one enters, is probably the oldest part of the church (it has been dated 1350). Overhead are two vaults with two bosses, one showing the martyrdom of St Stephen, and the other St Laurence rescuing a soul from demons.

The interior of St Stephen's is impressive. Its splendid hammer-beam roof progresses without break from end to end of the church, for there is no chancel arch. The continuous ranges of clerestory windows rest upon walls of panelled stone, the arches of the arcades are strongly moulded, and the supporting piers made more slender by the hollowing out of their surfaces.

A closer inspection of the roof reveals that the wall posts towards the eastern end rest on angel corbels, while the remaining corbels are plain; there are also changes in the wall panelling and in the spandrels of the beams. According to Sir St John Hope this point of change to angel corbels marks the meeting of the chancel (of 1530) and the nave (of 1550), the place where the rood screen crossed the nave and aisles.

The great east window contains a curious mixture of fifteenth- and sixteenth-century stained glass, the effect of which is very fine. There are scattered pieces of English glass, and several large figure subjects (dated 1511) from Germany. Another date (1601), prominently displayed in the window, is said to have no significance whatever.

Most of the windows suffered damage during the last war, and have been restored and repaired by G. King and Son, of Norwich. Others have been installed since, and their use of coloured subjects on a white ground makes an interesting comparison with those of earlier date. The west window lost all its glass (of 1865), excepting the little figures in the tracery, but there is a very good window of 1904, in memory of the Reverend James Wilson (by C. E. Kempe). In a window of the north aisle are the Royal Arms and those of Jane Seymour; the window nearby in memory of Joseph Massingham (1938) is by Knowles, of York. The recent windows by Alfred Wilkinson in the north aisle and transept are very good indeed.

In the restoration of 1859 the church was re-seated, and pews and pulpit date from that time. The work was well done. The pews have a variety of handsome poppy-heads and most of the pew ends still bear the little cast-iron plates that give their number or state that they are 'Free'. There are contrasts of furnishing in the choir, where one finds a pulpit of 1859 which is good, a brass lectern of about 1870 which is anything but, and four old stalls. Before the 1859 restoration the organ had stood upon a gallery in front of the west window; both had been there since 1814. The gallery was destroyed, and the organ replaced by a new instrument which was housed in the north transept. This fine organ (by Lewis, of London), now equipped with a detached console, is the one which stands at the east end of the north aisle. Behind the altar, a curtain hides an interesting reredos which may be a survival from the Georgian interior. On it the Creed, Commandments, and the Lord's Prayer are spelled out in Gothic letters, on zinc panels set in a Gothic frame.

The many wall tablets vary in style and date, from the praying figures of John Mingay and his wife (1617), to the kneeling lady upon the memorial erected to Lady Bignold in 1860.

Of eighteenth-century tablets, the finest is that by John Ivory to Charles and Mary Mackerell (1727), with the fish upon their coat of arms. There are monuments to sheriffs and aldermen, apothecaries, attorneys, silk mercers, stone masons, and a soldier.

Memorials to members of the medical profession reflect the church's long association with the Norfolk and Norwich Hospital. One who worked there, John Manning, a physician who died in 1806, is described as being 'A scholar without pride, a Christian without bigotry, and devout without ostentation'.

But the most curious tablet is that to Elizabeth Coppin (died 1812), in which the upper part is completely classical in spirit with a weeping cherub beside an urn, while the lower part assumes a form which is supposedly Gothic. It is the only memorial in Norwich of Coade stone, an artificial stone made in Lambeth by Coade and Sealy between 1769 and 1837. There is a tablet of this material in St Andrew's church, Thorpe (to Elizabeth Meadows Martineau, 1810). The figures on Yarmouth's Nelson Column are of Coade stone, as is the famous lion which used to stand upon the Thameside brewery at Lambeth.

In the chancel are several good brasses. They are to Ellen Buttrey, who died in 1546, to Thomas Bokenham (1460), to Dr Thomas Cappe, Vicar of St Stephens 1520 to 1545, to Richard Brasyer and his son (who was Mayor in 1510), and to Robert Brasyer and his wife (about 1510).

St Swithin

THE street we now call St Benedict's can scarcely have been free from the sound of masons' hammers during the whole of the fifteenth century when the churches there were being built. Those on the north side follow each other in such quick succession as to become confusing to the visitor.

Walking westwards one sees, beyond the church of St Laurence, the tower of St Margaret's a mere hundred yards away. Once there, the bell-turret of a third church appears, that of St Swithin's, only fifty yards further west.

A plain flint church without a tower, St Swithin's presents its southern side to the street. A small churchyard slopes down to it, although not so steeply here, for the river valley is opening out towards Dereham Road. A passage on the west leads round to the church's northern side; the tower which stood in this passage was condemned as unsafe by the then city engineer in 1882, and taken down. (Sillett's drawing of 1820 shows it to have been of medium height, unbuttressed, and with lean-to porches on north and south.) Today, the church has a pretty bell-turret upon its western gable, a roof that runs continuously from end to end, clerestory windows that are small, square-headed and wide apart, and aisles with Decorated windows and a priest's door on the south.

The north side of the church provides a complete surprise. It has the same clerestory windows as on the south, the aisle is the same save that a broad rood-stair turret is attached to it (with a sound-hole from the vanished tower built into it), but the mission hall is as large as the church itself. Its walls are of flint and brick, and its roof of tiles is attached to the eastern end of the aisle and stands at right-angles to it. It has large school-like windows, a large entrance door, and a path that leads to it across a square of churchyard, entered under a lamp suspended in an iron archway – all looking very nineteenth century and very Gothic. The hall is the work of the architect Herbert J. Green, and its date is 1908.

To tell how it came to be built one must go back to the turn of the century when St Swithin's was a small slum parish, where some 1,100 inhabitants dwelt in conditions which provided little light or air. Below the churchyard, St Swithin's Alley threaded its way, the only way, through a mass of close-packed property to Westwick Street.

Of all this the only building that remains is the charming thatched house (then two cottages) that stands in the corner where the alley curved round the churchyard, next to which was the well-known Hampshire Hog. Across the alley, houses circled the churchyard, among them the old rectory, by then a poor tenement house.

The church had been closed since 1891, and its condition was well described by a newspaper correspondent who wrote, 'Of all the churches in Norwich doomed to ruin, St Swithin's has lain longest in bad condition. Indeed, so bad has it been of late that it has been difficult to persuade some who have surveyed its desolation from the top of a tram-car that it is a church at all.' That was in 1905, and four years later the same newspaper, under the headline 'A notable restoration', was able to announce that the little church had been fully repaired, and a mission hall built against its northern side.

All this was due to the enthusiasm of a young clergyman, the Reverend John Sawbridge, who had been Rector of the parish for little more than a year, and to the generosity of an anonymous acquaintance. The Rector guided the fortunes of the parish until 1922, and on a visit some thirty years later – by which time the population had dwindled to one hundred and, sadly, the church was again closed – he told how the church had been restored and the hall built, how the anonymous gentleman had come to visit the church in his company, how he, as Rector, had been called away to baptise a dying child, and how the visitor, while waiting, had been so moved by the poverty he had seen around him that he had promised, then and there, not only to restore the church, but to provide a social centre, where these people could meet and enjoy what leisure they had in pleasant surroundings.

In plan St Swithin's is a rectangle with a tiny sanctuary added to the east end. There is no chancel division but the rood-stair opening shows where the medieval screen once crossed nave and aisles. The aisle arcades are most unusual – those on the north consisting of a range of classical piers and arches (of about 1700), while those on the south have their original pointed arches and fifteenth-century piers. The Georgian doorcase at the western end originally stood under a deep gallery which stretched across the nave. This was complete with panelled front and clock, and was entered from the tower staircase.

There are some good tablets upon the walls. In the sanctuary is one of about 1650 to Anne Scottowe, with a quaint cherub head below it in unusually high relief. One by Thomas Rawlins in the south aisle is to a merchant, William Wilcocks, who died in 1770 and who 'notwithstanding his labouring under a total deprivation of sight for many years, he supported it with great cheerfulness'. But perhaps the best is the large tablet by T. Stafford to Abraham Robertson, who died in 1777.

The church hall must have been a splendid place in its heyday; its well-lit main room extends under a curved ceiling to a stage at the northern end, and behind this is a further wing which contained clubrooms and kitchens (where parishioners sought refuge during the floods of 1912).

After many sad years of use as a furniture store, St Swithin's (now in the hands of Norwich Historic Churches Trust) has become Norwich Arts Centre, the church serving as the concert hall, and the mission hall providing the restaurant, exhibition space and offices. And so a new and vital artistic spirit has been breathed into the old edifice.

The church and mission hall from the north

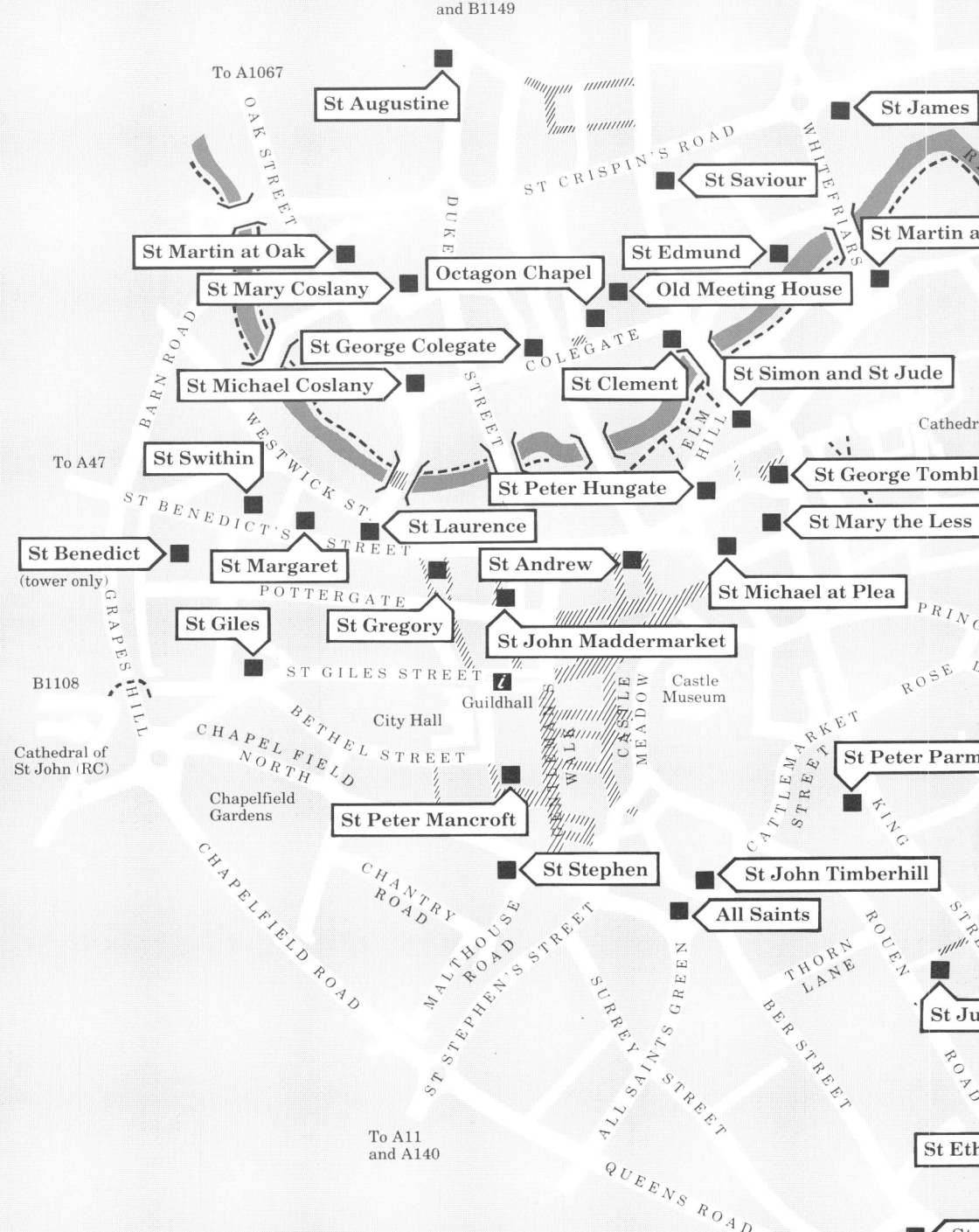